The
New
Adapters

Jacob Armstrong
with Adam Hamilton and Mike Slaughter

The
New
Adapters

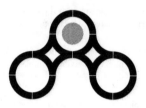

Shaping Ideas
to Fit Your Congregation

Abingdon Press™

Nashville

THE NEW ADAPTERS:
SHAPING IDEAS TO FIT YOUR CONGREGATION

Copyright © 2015 by Abingdon Press

This book is printed on acid-free paper.

Library of Congress Cataloging-in-Publication Data

Armstrong, Jacob (Pastor)
  The new adapters : shaping ideas to fit your congregation / Jacob Armstrong, with Adam Hamilton and
Mike Slaughter.—First [edition].
    pages cm.
  ISBN 978-1-63088-323-2 (binding : soft back : alk. paper)   1. Church renewal.   2. Church develop-
ment, New.   I. Title.
  BV600.3.A76 2015
  253–dc23
                                                                                  2014043359

All scripture quotations unless noted otherwise are from the Common English Bible. Copyright © 2011
by the Common English Bible. All rights reserved. Used by permission. www.CommonEnglishBible.com.

The section on Dr. George Tinker and repentance in chapter 2 (pp. 19–20) is excerpted and adapted from
the article "Y'all Continually Repent," which was previously published on MinistryMatters.com. All rights
reserved.

The names in the story of Chris, Stephanie, and their children (pp. 92–94) have been changed to protect
the identities of the subjects.

15 16 17 18 19 20 21 22 23 24—10 9 8 7 6 5 4 3 2 1
MANUFACTURED IN THE UNITED STATES OF AMERICA

To Rachel, my beautiful bride

CONTENTS

INTRODUCTION

"Your wife is ugly."

I looked around. He was talking to me.

"Your wife is ugly." I was at first confused, then, pretty quickly, offended.

Let me back up. I had recently been invited to join a covenant group with some other pastors from across the country. Our first few meetings had been online but we were now gathered for our first face-to-face meeting. We had been discussing some of the issues facing the church. The tone had grown critical and cynical, as we had begun to do the easy work of pointing out all the things wrong with the twenty-first-century church in America. We had a lot of material to choose from, including examples from our own denomination and our own congregations. We were clever, we were cute, and we were cutting the church down. Like I said, it was easy. As pastors who spend the bulk of our time in the church world, we were expertly qualified to point out the faults of the people of God. It came natural to us; it was almost as if we enjoyed it.

Somewhere in the midst of that conversation, John, a pastor from North Carolina I had grown to admire in our web meetings, said the unthinkable. And he said it to me: "Your wife is ugly." Number one, he had never met my wife. Number two, my wife is gorgeous (pictured below—just kidding). Number three, where I come from that type of insult results in a throw-down. Because I didn't respond, he said it again. I looked around the table hoping to draw some context clues from the others on how I should respond. They looked as confused as I did.

John didn't let the awkwardness linger long. "Isn't this what we say to Jesus when we talk this way about the church?" Suddenly, we all knew what he was saying. The Bible refers to the church as Jesus's bride. For Jesus, the church is a thing of beauty. Jesus loves the church and considers himself to be one flesh with it. And here we were saying how ugly she was. John made his point. And I was still a little mad at him.

Do we believe that Jesus still looks at the church as a thing of beauty? If so, should this affect how we talk about her?

A predominantly negative rhetoric exists around the church today. For many on the outside of the church, "judgmental" and "hypocritical" are the first words that come to mind when asked about Christ's body. Many more on the outside have moved on from thinking negatively to something worse. They don't talk about the church at all. Apathy has grown. Instead of turning their noses up to the church, they walk by without even noticing.

But it is those of us who are a part of the church that are best at pointing out its blemishes. Pastors gather for coffee and gripe. Laypeople church-hop from one congregation to the next, finding the new one as broken and bruised as the last. We cleverly blog about the latest dumb thing the church has done, all the while shining a spotlight on how cute we are and casting the bride of Christ further into the shadows.

This book will not be about calling Jesus's bride ugly. Instead my hope is that it shines light on her beauty, a beauty that still stops me in my tracks. For sure, we have to be real about the ugly. Jesus didn't shy away from calling out the religious ugliness of his day. But his eyes were always on the horizon. He looked to a new day when the kingdom would come and the church would be made right. He looked to it in the future, and he claimed it in the present. I think we should do the same.

It should be known that I love the church. I imagine that you might too. Maybe a better way of saying it is, **I believe in the church**. That confession is tucked in toward the end of our historic creed, but it is one that we should reclaim. As I hear my generation claim a faith in Jesus but decry the church, I think we should be reminded that we only know about Jesus because of the church. Broken, blemished, and battered for sure, it has carried the story for all these centuries.

I believe in the church. I was baptized in a little white dress in a small Methodist church in 1980. I was four months old while my twenty-something parents held me, made promises for me, loved me, and did what they thought was right and holy.

The more I learn about the event, the more I realize that it was the most important one of my life. It's strange I know; something that I had no control over, no decision in, no memory of…guides me still today.

I have learned now that my family was a disconnected family, disconnected from God and the church. My dad grew up in a fundamental church in Tennessee in the 1950s and '60s. If he asked questions, he was given black-and-white answers. When he inquired about the gray areas of the time (think assassinations, racial prejudice, and confusing wars) he was given not space but rebuke. Guilt motivated salvation, and by the time he was eighteen he was running from the church as he knew it as fast as he could. My mother, on the other hand, did not grow up attending church. She grew up in a large, close family that frequently moved and never settled into regular church attendance. And yet sometime in the late 1970s, as a young married couple, just starting a family, my parents met someone who became a friend, who they trusted, who then simply invited them to St. Paul's United Methodist Church, a church start just getting its legs underneath it. My mother and older brother were baptized, and then a short time later, I was baptized, and something in the heart of that young family began to desire deeply to know more of Jesus Christ. We had this insatiable Jesus-pull on our life. We hungered for him, not knowing the rules, not knowing all the appropriate behaviors, and that church gave us space to seek him.

I think about how my baptism in that newly built sanctuary changed the course of my history, and I'm so thankful for the church. Infant baptism is a symbol that God is working in the heart of a child long before he or she can make a reciprocal effort to love and choose God. Infant baptism puts more emphasis on the action of God than the action of the boy or girl. Infant baptism is a hopeful precursor to the day when the child answers the wooing longing desire of God to be connected, to be in relationship. And on the day I was baptized:

My parents repented of their sin and acknowledged the power God gives to release them from sin.

They professed their faith in Jesus as Savior and Lord.

And interestingly in the ancient liturgy of the church, they professed their belief in the church that God has opened to people of all ages, nations, and races.

Then they made a promise over me. This young couple who had been disconnected from the church promised to pray for me, teach me about Jesus, and bring me to church until I was old enough to choose Jesus myself.

And they fulfilled their promise.

So, I have some hesitation with the whole "we like Jesus, but not the church" concept that many of my generation have purported over the last several years. I mean, I get it. I spend every day in some way connected to the church, and most days I like Jesus a lot more than I like the church. But I have begun to wonder, is this really an option—Jesus without the church?

Is there really a Jesus without the church?

Jesus, like us, was critical of the established religion of his day, but would he go for that?

"Yeah, you can just have me; you don't need to gather with the rest of these messed-up people."

I think the answer is no. Simply and clearly, no.

I am still considered a young clergyperson in the denomination in which I serve. I am often asked, "Why did you get into this?" The reason: I believe in the church. Not just Jesus. I could have lived out my vocation in a different way if it was just about me and him. But it's bigger than that.

I can't shake that had it not been for the vision of some people in a living room in the early 1970s saying we need a new church in this new community to reach new people, had it not been for a young pastor who took an appointment that was not glamorous, then my parents wouldn't have heard the story again and for the first time. I wouldn't have learned in the way that I did that Jesus loved me. And it all happened in the church. Not in a building, but in the church.

So, the church wasn't second or third on my list. I saw it then, and see it still today, as the best thing going. And while I will make no defense for some of the horrendous, hateful things the church has done, and though I will at times be critical of some of the thoughtless, lazy ways the church has grown complacent, I want to be clear: I love the church. And I believe in it.

I also believe the church won't fail. I often hear that the church is dying. This statement is largely based on the analysis of data that shows the number of worshipping people in churches in America is declining (and it has been for quite some time). Studies show that if these attendance and conversion trends continue, many of our mainline denominations will be facing certain death. Certainly "the church is dying" would make no sense in large pockets of church growth in South America and Africa. "The church is dying" would bewilder the faithful Christian church in China, a church that has grown exponentially over the last century, largely in illegal house churches. It should also be mentioned that there are churches in America that are experiencing life and growth in ways that are both inspiring and beautiful. But on the whole, American churches are on hospice care. Symptoms are being treated to make the church comfortable as she slowly dies. She dies while the communities that surround these old, large buildings grow more and more disconnected to and disinterested in what is taking place inside of them. Urban areas in most large American cities feature dilapidated church buildings that may be home to twenty worshipping people with white skin in an otherwise colorful neighborhood. Many more of these former houses of worship are boarded up or now occupied by more successful business ventures. The neighborhood has changed, but the church hasn't. And it is dying.

But death is not the destiny of Jesus's church. Much of our anxiety in the church centers on our concern that we will lose the church. We may lose the church as we know it, but the church won't die. Why? It is dependent on God, not us. It is fueled by God's Spirit, not our effort or ingenuity.

But, *the church has to change*. It has to adapt to a culture that finds it repulsive or, even worse, irrelevant. We can't continue to do the things my church did in the 1980s to reach families in our community because families in our communities are different than they were in the 1980s. Most churches are still using a model from the 1950s (or 1850s)— you get the point.

This book is about a group of people, both clergy and lay, who love the church and who know the church has to change. We will call them New Adapters. New Adapters are people carrying on an old tradition of adapting the timeless story of Jesus to a changing cultural landscape. New Adapters love the church, believe it won't fail, but know it has to change. I'm guessing that you might fit this description as well. I will share with you stories of New Adapters in the pages to come, and we will shine light on a church that is alive.

I was fortunate to connect with Adam Hamilton and Mike Slaughter the same fall that I helped start Providence Church. Adam and Mike inspired me because they were still passionate about the church after some years in. I had seen many pastors who, after a couple of decades, had become either cynical and jaded or burned out and just counting their days until retirement. In fact, my wife, Rachel, and I noted that as we met with pastor after pastor to seek to learn from them that many had either become hardened and angry at the church or had been relegated to a "quivering mass of availability" (to use a term by Richard Lischer in *Open Secrets: A Memoir of Faith and Discovery* [New York: Broadway Books, 2001], 67). We desired something different.

I saw something different in Mike and Adam. They seemed to burn brighter as each year went on; they seemed to have more hope for the church than they did even when they started. They understood that serving in the church was difficult, both of them receiving their share of bumps and bruises along the way. Yet, they still believed in the church. They loved the church.

Their stories were different: Adam starting a new church in Kansas City; Mike taking over an old, rural church just outside of Dayton. And yet, their stories were the same. They remained committed to a vision to reach those who felt disconnected from God and the church, families like mine. Adam calls them nonreligious and nominally religious people and has seen tens of thousands of them connect with Jesus at Church of the Resurrection. Mike, who was sent to a dying church in a dying city, saw new life in amazing ways (God does God's best work in graveyards, Mike says) as Ginghamsburg Church went from a small rural church to one of the leading churches in the nation in terms of serving the poor both domestically and globally.

As I heard Mike and Adam share as a part of a mentoring network they established with young clergy, I felt at once inspired and overwhelmed. The things they talked about moved me, but they also initially seemed unrealistic for me because their contexts were so different from mine. Middle Tennessee shared little with the area around Dayton. A new church of just a few dozen had little in common with a megachurch of thousands. And yet, as they shared I began to hear the heartbeat of their two different, yet similar, churches. As they shared their stories, I saw clearly common threads that ran throughout. No one would confuse their churches, in fact no one would confuse Adam with Mike, but as they talked I heard the same message of unyielding commitment to a vision that I believe Jesus would recognize.

I wondered if the principles that they shared could be applied in my unique setting.

I found that they could.

The vision would be the same (reaching the disconnected); the actual approach would have to fit my mission field.

This is what we hope to share in this book. Adam and Mike will share how they have led churches that have remained unashamedly committed to reaching those who feel disconnected from God and the church. I will share how our new church has taken these principles and applied them to our context and how you might do the hard work of applying tried and true best practices to your unique setting and context. Adam and Mike will share wisdom for pastors and church leaders who still believe in the church as God's designed vessel for sharing the Jesus story with the world. We will seek to change the rhetoric that it is best to put the mainline church on hospice care and watch it die a graceful death. We know the church won't die, and the amazing thing is...we get to be a part of it!

At the age of twenty-seven, I was given the opportunity to start a church for those who feel disconnected from God and the church. Just a couple months in as a pastor of a church with no name, no people, and no place to meet, I met Nicole. Nicole told me right off the bat that she didn't have any interest in the church. She said she felt close to God or some greater power in nature, but Jesus she didn't know much about.

Rachel invited her over for dinner.

It turns out, the more she heard about Jesus, the more she wanted to know about Jesus. I invited her to come to Providence Church once the congregation began meeting, no strings attached—just come and hear about him. She came.

Week after week after week.

Her first child was born that summer. Mya Jane. And on a sunny, windy day in September in an elementary school gym, Mya was baptized as an infant in a little white dress. And Nicole was baptized too.

She repented of her sin.

She professed her belief in Jesus.

And part of the ancient ritual called upon her to say she would serve Jesus in union with the church.

The church that Christ opened to all people.

It's hard work to be an adapter. It's easier to do the same things we've done and hope for different results. It's even easier to join the downward spiral of negativity and ride the cynicism wherever it goes. Many more will join you in that exercise than in the prayerful, discerning work of adapting the unchanging message of life to a world that didn't wait to tell us it was changing yet again.

But trust me on this. My wife is not ugly and the bride of Christ is not ugly. And when we shine light on the beauty of Christ and his church, it is worth every effort we can give.

The New Adapters Diagram

The New Adapters image will be a way of thinking about the models of ministry that you have encountered (both good and bad) and how through prayerful discernment you can adapt those to meet the unique needs of the communities you serve. It is hard, but necessary, work that leaders must do. We take the effective strategies and ideas that we see in other contexts and adapt them to our own.

In each chapter, then, you'll see this diagram illustrating the shift from the established ideas and methods that have worked for churches in the past (the left bubble) to the new adaptation (the top bubble). The diagram doesn't show linear steps but marks a progression from those established ideas to the new adaptation proposed in this book.

The right bubble then demonstrates the ways churches are currently trying to improve, our current reality. The new adaptation in each chapter will be exemplified by illustrations from current pastors across the country.

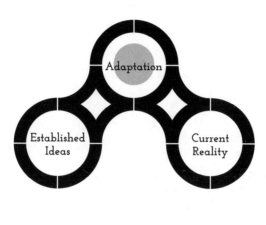

A Conversation with Adam Hamilton and Mike Slaughter

On an evening in the fall of 2014, I gathered with Adam Hamilton and Mike Slaughter to discuss our hope for the church and how the concepts shared in this book might be helpful for others seeking to adapt God's timeless message to different and changing contexts. We were joined by New Adapters DJ Del Rosario, Lia McIntosh, and Mark Sheets. At the end of each chapter will be a section entitled "A Conversation with Adam and Mike," where Adam and Mike's thoughts and insights from that night are captured. Enjoy the honest and fresh reflections of two practitioners who for years now have done the difficult adaptive work described in this book and still believe in the church.

To watch the videos and view photographs from the New Adapter conversation with Adam and Mike, visit http://www.jacob-armstrong .com.

Chapter One

THE VISION MUST FIT THE MISSION FIELD

God called me to be a missionary.

And then sent me to suburbia.

I was just sure God had somewhere exotic for me. Somewhere that would require one of those planes that land in the water to get there. I would probably have to wear an Indiana Jones hat. A beard would be a must. Rachel and I applied with a mission organization. We flew to Monterrey, Mexico, and saw where our placement would be. We cried as we considered how God might use us to reach that city with the love of Jesus.

We came home and told our parents, our kids, and our church that God was calling us to Mexico.

Then it all fell apart.

Everything that needed to happen for us to be able to go to Mexico unraveled before our eyes. Funding, language school admittance, denominational permissions. No, no, no.

I was confused.

Shortly after our last no (or not right now), I flew to the Church of the Resurrection for a denominational conference. While there I was approached by some leaders from my home conference who asked me if I had heard of the new church that was being proposed back in Tennessee.

I had not.

It would be in the Providence area of Mt. Juliet, a new urbanism development that would double the size of the city. "Have you heard of the area?" they asked.

I had. It was my hometown.

Then they told me I was being considered as the pastor to start it. I was confused.

I got in my rented minivan (I drive a minivan all the time now, but back then it was a novelty) and went for a drive. I still remember the exit that I took off the interstate: Gardner, Kansas.

I pulled over and in a cornfield on the side of the road got on my knees and prayed. (I know it sounds *Field of Dreams*-ish; it was really kind of itchy.)

Why? I wondered. Why would God do all this missionary stuff in my heart? Why would God break my heart for Monterrey, Mexico? Why all of this if I am to go to my hometown and start a new church?

I heard God's voice in my heart say, *Because I wanted you to have that heart for your town. I wanted you to cry over that city and instead you were on your way to becoming a fairly average religious professional.* Well, I'm not sure God said it exactly like that, but that's what I heard.

Three months later I had moved and was the pastor of a new church with no name, no place to meet, and, oh yeah, no people.

It was a city that looked much different from Monterrey, Mexico. Financial poverty was harder to find; spiritual poverty was rampant. They spoke my language if I mean English, but they didn't speak Christianese or all the other church languages I had studied for so long. The people looked a lot like me, but they were diverse in the way they viewed God and in their experience of church.

What I realized is that I would have to learn from and listen to the people of Mt. Juliet, Tennessee, in much the same way I would have learned from and listened to the people of a foreign land.

I learned that I did in fact bring many preconceived notions of what they needed and what I wanted in a church. I learned that I knew them only slightly better than I knew the people of Monterrey, Mexico. I learned that a danger in church work is creating a church in my mind and assuming that it will fit the mission field to which I am assigned by God (and my denomination). I learned that no matter how savvy, well-read, and well-trained I may be, there is no substitute to learning, knowing, and loving the community to which I have been sent. The vision has to fit the mission field. I would have never dreamed of creating a worship service or a church experience in Mexico that fit my preferences. The music would have been indigenous, the dress would have fit the culture, and the language would have been understandable to the people of that place. Things that would in no way compromise the message would be shaped to fit the context. Adaptive work would be essential.

It is strange, then, that we regularly skip that step when we try to do ministry in areas where people look like us. One of the biggest mistakes I find in working with church planters and those starting new ministries in existing churches is when we create a vision that fits our preferences and likes and ignores those we are really trying to reach.

This usually happens when we skip the important step of listening to and learning from our community and simply create a cool experience for those we already have.

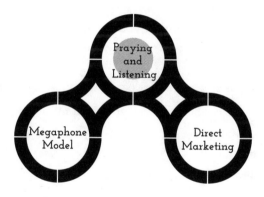

Listening to and Learning from Your Community

The vision must fit the mission field, and the first step to having this congruity is **prayer**. We must begin by asking God to show us what he sees in the communities to which we have been sent. When we get serious about reaching our communities, it is tempting to forget to pray. There is so much to do and there seems to be little time to do it in. When we become New Adapters who are willing to take risks and be courageous, one of the first things we often do is seek out ideas from the experts. We read the hottest books in *church growth*, *missional church*, *evangelism*—or whatever word is the buzz at the time—categories (thanks for reading this book by the way). We attend the conferences of the leading churches that we admire (this, too, is a good idea). And we forget to pray, like really pray.

First we should pray, and pray together. Nothing will substitute for a season of prayer among a group of Jesus followers who want to see God work in and transform their community. I am reminded of Nehemiah's prayer before he went to Jerusalem to rebuild the wall. Before he gathered his team and discussed tactics. Before he went to the king to ask permission. Before any of the action, he prayed. He mourned and fasted and prayed. There is no substitute for that spiritual work. It aligns our hearts and our ears and our eyes with what God wants us to do. So before you plan your worship service, before you discuss what to name it and who your drummer will be, ask God to give you a vision for your community and then ask God to give you ears to listen to your community. If possible, do this with a team of people who likewise want to see the church prevail in your town. I recommend these questions coming out of that season of prayer and discovery:

- What unique opportunities does your community present?
- What unique challenges does your community present?
- What are the hopes and dreams of the people in your community?
- What is breaking their hearts?
- What is breaking God's heart?
- What is unique about what you (your church) have to offer to your community?

When we were forming the people who would become Providence Church, we spent some time listening. Some months. Before we talked about worship style or where we would meet or what we would be called (exciting things that can be very distracting in forming something new), we listened.

We walked through the grocery store and through the neighborhoods on Sunday mornings at 10:00 a.m. (the hour most churches in the area met). If we truly wanted to reach people who weren't in church, well then who were these people and what were they doing? We rolled our windows down at the stoplights and listened to what type of music they were listening to. (Surprisingly, we heard no organ music. I know, it hurts.)

I learned quickly that my community wasn't as trendy as I had originally envisioned my new church to be. If I had mentally designed a cutting-edge church (and I had) in music, dress, and appearance, then I had been sent to the wrong place. I was not in a reclaimed urban area where hipsters were buying old run-down homes and visiting farmer's markets. I was in suburban America, where soccer and minivans abound (yes, I bought one). As we began to pray for and over our community, our hearts were turned toward who they were, not what we wanted to do.

Before we choose our tactics, we have to listen. The church planter from the 1980s will tell you to knock on every door in the neighborhood. The 1990s church growth expert would have you gather two dozen people to call everyone in the phone book. The early 2000s pastor would swear by the mass mailing that sends tens of thousands of postcards with smiling faces on them to every mailbox. Today, many neighborhoods prohibit soliciting, people don't have a home phone, and most of us throw away junk mail without looking at it. This is not to say these strategies shouldn't be employed, but learn your community before you start wasting time and money. All of these tactics have the same beautiful goal at heart: reaching new people for Christ and connecting them with the church we still believe in. But the difficult work you have been given is discovering how this can be done in your unique context.

I think this may be the most important work that New Adapters do. There was a time when the church sought to have the biggest voice in the community. We built a big sanctuary so everyone could hear our theologically sound preaching. We even built schools where all the children of the community could come. We had long hallways of educational space for adults so they could hear our sound doctrine. Today, though, I believe a key adaptation for a church that appears to be dying will be to move from the megaphone model of ministry where we are speaking all the right things to our people to putting the megaphone in our ear and listening real hard to what the people are saying. Of course what we have to say is of critical importance, but there come times when key adaptations are needed, and now is a time where listening must come first. Thomas Edison coined the term *megaphone* in 1878 with a new device to benefit the deaf and hard of hearing. The first megaphone was actually three funnels. Two funnels that were over six feet long were inserted in the ear to aid hearing. The third, a smaller one, fit the mouth to project the voice. We must move our megaphone from our mouths to our ears, at least long enough to hear what the people are saying.

In our listening and learning process we looked at **demographic studies**. It is not hard to acquire pages and pages of information on your community. These are not without merit. We learned that 33 percent of the people in our community are eighteen and under. This would shape how we thought about church and what we would do to reach out to our community. Make sure you include this type of study in your learning and listening stage, but don't stop there.

The true discovery of your context will not be found in a printout; it will be found as you live and breathe in it. **Spend time in the coffee shops and beyond.** Quick caution here: most of the time the people hanging out in coffee shops are pastors. Usually when I try to spark conversation with someone in a coffee shop who I think might be a prospect for our church, the potential convert ends up being a pastor! But the idea of visiting the "third places" in our community is key to learning your context. Every community has places for informal gathering outside the workplace and the home. Seek these places out. It may be the dog park, the softball fields, or the breakfast café. You need to know these places and frequent them. We still take time to send our staff out to our third places to listen and take notes. What do people look like? How do they dress? What are they talking about? Eavesdrop!

I often find church planters paralyzed by the idea of hanging out in coffee shops and trying to grow a church by meeting people in public places. While I recommend being friendly and learning the names of the folks you encounter in your community, I don't think walking up to a stranger in Starbucks is the best way to meet new people. In a changing culture, New Adapters have to learn the best ways to encounter new people and form real relationships that lead to deep connections.

We must take the time to form the kinds of relationships that allow us to invite people to encounter God.

A great way of doing this is **identifying and meeting with people of peace**. This technique employed in African church planting today is adapted from the teaching of Jesus about going out into the community and listening. When Jesus sent out the Seventy-Two into the neighborhoods to knock on doors and hand out brochures about the church (or something like that), he recommended looking for people of peace. "*Whenever you enter a house, first say, 'May peace be on this house.' If anyone there shares God's peace, then your peace will rest on that person. If not, your blessing will return to you. Remain in this house, eating and drinking whatever they set before you*" (Luke 10:5-7a). Instead of standing on the corner with a megaphone preaching in the hopes of drawing a crowd, look for people who, as Jesus says, "share God's peace." Every community has them. People who are connected with others in a peaceful way. Our church grew rapidly when we connected with one person who immediately connected us with twelve more. One example was connecting with the leader of a local moms' group. This group met once a week for much-needed socialization for the mothers and play for the young children. These are the types of interactions that many new moms find in their church home. The moms' group was mostly women who didn't have a church home. Connecting with just one young mother in this group led to a dozen eventually coming to our church. You will learn about your community from the people of peace, the connectors, the leaders in your community. Find them, spend time with them, learn from them.

We also learn about our community by **learning from other churches**. No doubt there are other churches in your community that are being effective in reaching people. As we will discuss later in the book, we can't ignore the opportunities we have to connect with other Christians in our community. You can learn from them what they have already learned. You can learn why a Saturday service won't work or why a ministry to single people is a must.

There are many ways to listen to and learn from your community. These are just a few. But before we think about ways to shape ministry and adapt, we have to understand who we are trying to reach.

In short, we can't out-cool ourselves by becoming intoxicated on cutting-edge ideas or ministries that appeal to us. I often see Mike preach in jeans, Adam in a robe, and Olu Brown in a coat and tie. The message coming out of their mouths is the same. But they have been careful to adapt themselves to speak in a way that people can understand.

Olu Brown founded Impact Church in Atlanta in 2007. Atlanta had no lack of churches, but what Olu and his team sought to do was different. In fact, "doing church differently" became a mantra for them as they sought to reach people who weren't currently in church while also seeking to transform the community. What impressed me so much about Olu and Impact was their deep desire to reach people in their community where they are. They did not construct a church that fit their ideals and preferences but instead did the difficult work of carefully crafting worship, outreach events, and discipleship ministries that fit their unique urban Atlanta context. Impact does a lot of innovative and fun ministry, but their desire to do things differently really is the desire to do whatever it takes to reach the people God has called them to reach. This means that no matter where they have met, a public school, a major conference center, and now their beautifully renovated building, they have kept the vision that was forged through careful listening to and participation in the city of Atlanta.

As a church planter, Lia McIntosh had a vision in her mind of the kind of church she wanted to start in Kansas City. After coming to the community, though, and learning the needs of the people, she realized her expectations would have to change. After worshipping in a gym for nine months and hosting community outreach events—carnivals, sports programs, festivals, and so on—Lia found that people weren't showing up for church. Hundreds would come to a community event, but nobody came to her church. They would say, "We love your events, but where is your church?" "Well," she would say, "Church is right here in the gym." But they didn't feel it. For them, church could not be church in a school gym, no matter what Lia did to church up the environment. The congregation finally relocated into an existing church building where the congregation had dwindled and the church had been closed. The building was gifted to the new church. Then— finally—people started to show up. Lia says the biggest lesson they learned was they had "to be humble and willing to not have all the answers." My church has grown in school gyms, but Lia's context called for something different. Because she listened, she was able to adapt to reach the people in her community.

So, we must take the vision that we feel God has given us (our *hopes and dreams for ministry*) and the reality of the context that we learn from a season of listening (*contextual reality*) and discern a faithful purpose for our work there (a *vision that fits the mission field*).

Obviously this involves letting go of the image you had of your ministry before you arrived where you serve. It means letting go of the preconceived picture you had of how it would go. It means embracing the place where God has placed you now. But when the vision fits the mission field it is sweet. You see people respond to the message of life found only in Jesus Christ. And as we open ourselves up to what God wants, our hearts change.

One morning on my drive through my suburban neighborhood, I found myself crying. Crying over the city. I knew I was in the right spot.

A Conversation with Adam and Mike

Mike: When I went to Ginghamsburg, the area was mostly rural. I knew that over 70 percent were unchurched. I liked rock music and pop culture, so I determined that I might be able to reach the people who were turned off by the kind of church I was turned off by—the sort of church that didn't understand or accept the culture of that time. So I started the kind of church that would reach the people in the area who were not being reached by any church. We grew with mostly twenty-somethings and thirtysomethings. And after about ten years, older people began to trust us as a church. But everything changes! All these years I'd been focusing on people in their twenties, thirties, and forties, because that was the population around us. But increasingly it is older populations that are a growing demographic for us. So the mission field changes all the time as neighborhoods change, as communities change.

Adam: When we started Resurrection the average age in the area was thirty-five. We looked at the churches that had started in the community and they were all Willow Creek—style churches doing exclusively contemporary worship services. People in this community were mostly in upper-middle-income brackets and highly educated. We recognized that most of those folks hadn't grown up going to a Willow Creek–style church, so that style was not what they thought of as "church." Instead, most of the people in our area had some experience from childhood in a traditional-style church. We could see that the one unfilled niche for church in this community was traditional worship with traditional music, so we started Resurrection with an intentional decision to do something that was different from everyone else. We recruited a small choir, played the organ, sang hymns, used traditional music, incorporated some historical liturgy, said the Lord's Prayer, and sang the doxology. And I wore a pulpit robe, which gave me a look of credibility since I was only twenty-five! It wasn't my preferred style perhaps, but that approach to worship and church is what connected with the nonreligious and nominally religious people in the community at the time. They were willing to come—and to return—because what we were doing felt familiar to them. But we also tried every week to infuse the service with a sense of the Spirit's power and to show how our faith has relevance to their daily lives and how it has real meaning. The first three services we developed at Resurrection were all traditional. We only added contemporary worship when, four years later, we needed to draw people away from an overcrowded traditional morning service. And today our largest attended service is still the choir and orchestra-led service.

Mike: We must be incarnational. The population in Dayton is around 140,000, and the area has lost 40,000 people in the last few decades. Since 2008 we have lost 34,000 manufacturing jobs. More and more people in our area are the struggling, urban, blue collar, working poor. It is a different community than it was thirty years ago. So how does the church change as the community around it changes? The church must never be static. It must always be incarnational and dynamic.

Adam: That's right. We must understand the communities we are in, and we must be able to do what it takes in order to reach different people in different places. For instance, our campuses all feel very different from one another. Downtown is different from Blue Springs, which is different from Leawood, and our West campus is something else entirely. Each has a unique flavor specific to the context of its community.

And each one is reaching the non- and nominally religious people in those communities.

Part of our task is getting to know the people in the community. Part of it is the leader's intuition, too. You have to have a sense of what really connects with the people in your community. For all our services, including the contemporary ones, we ask, "What is distinctively Wesleyan about this? What makes this a United Methodist worship service?" Worship at Resurrection doesn't look the same as at the nondenominational church down the street. Some of this relates to using inclusive language, making sure we are introducing social concerns in the context of worship, and combining grace and holiness. We might sing some of the songs in contemporary worship that everyone else is singing, but are there other songs that we could sing that are distinctively Wesleyan? Or can we rewrite a hymn to make it feel more right and more singable for people today but retain the Methodist approach in the lyrics?

Mike: Go into the neighborhood and ask what they need. We started with the local government and other institutions and organizations when we were starting our campuses in Dayton. We had been doing ministry in Trotwood, which is primarily an African American community, before we even opened the campus. I coached a four-year-old soccer team there, and my granddaughter played in that league. We spent time in that community and got a sense of the people and the needs. The library had two thousand books in the early education and children's section. We've facilitated book drives and other programs there, and now they have fourteen thousand books. There hadn't been fireworks on the Fourth of July in that community for twenty years, because the local government couldn't afford it based on the tax base. So we've done fireworks and a carnival in the neighborhood. Another thing we found when we talked to people and asked what they needed was a real need for housing. So we developed partnerships with other organizations and have built new houses. In part, this gets down to our theology: we believe the local church should be the empowering center of the neighborhood. So we strive to be that—to be the church that helps people, empowers people.

View photos and video clips from this conversation with Adam and Mike at http://www.jacob-armstrong.com.

Chapter Two

IT HAS TO BE GOOD
NEWS TO THE POOR

Jesus's ministry began with a season of preparation. Even Jesus needed a season of getting ready for the heavy lifting of changing the world forever. Forty days in the wilderness. He fasted, prayed, and faced temptation. Sounds great, huh?

The temptations he faced were not unlike the ones we face in ministry today. He was tempted with bread, representing a provision he had not enjoyed in quite a while. He was tempted with authority, power, and fame, still some of the devil's favorites with us. Jesus's third temptation was to put the power of God on display in a way that made a show out of what God could do.

Jesus refuted each temptation with a reminder to the devil and himself of God's word, which pointed his heart back to the true desire of God. Jesus remembered that all he needed was in God, that power and authority belonged only to God, and that the wonders of God were not to be used as a sideshow for our enjoyment. What Jesus experienced in his season in the desert prepared him for a short three-year season of ministry that seemed to have a laser-like focus.

In chapter 1 we discussed engaging in a season of preparation before stepping out in a focused manner. Our seasons of preparation will mirror Jesus's. As we said, it will involve the spiritual disciplines of prayer and fasting. It will also include temptation. There will be the temptation to throw in the towel and go after provisions we are not currently enjoying. We will be tempted to have authority, power, and fame. We may even be tempted to do things that make a show out of God and in so doing cheapen God's power. But as we engage and walk through these preparatory seasons, we will come through with a more focused purpose on the other side. A vision that fits the mission field.

Shortly after Jesus's season of preparation, he stood in the synagogue of Nazareth (his hometown) on the Sabbath and read from the prophet Isaiah.

He read:

> *The Spirit of the Lord is upon me,*
> > *because the Lord has anointed me.*
> *He has sent me to preach good news to the poor,*
> > *to proclaim release for the prisoners*
> > *and recovery of sight to the blind,*
> > *to liberate the oppressed,*
> > *and to proclaim the year of the Lord's favor. (Luke 4:18-19)*

It seems that Jesus must have emphasized the *mes* in this passage as if he were talking about himself. We know at the conclusion of the reading Jesus said, "Today, this scripture has been fulfilled just as you heard it" (Luke 4:21). And we know the people who heard him were ready to kill him.

After a season of listening and learning, Jesus announces his vision for his ministry. We should listen closely.

> *Good news to the poor.*
>
> *Release for the prisoners.*
>
> *Recovery of sight to the blind.*
>
> *Liberation for the oppressed.*

This, Jesus's first sermon, is often titled "The Beginning of the Galilean Ministry" (e.g., NRSV). Either that or "Jesus Rejected at Nazareth" (e.g., NIV and NLT). The unveiling of Jesus's vision was also the first time he was publicly and collectively rejected. Many of us will experience the same thing!

I will never forget sitting with a small group in the old Ginghamsburg Church building as Mike Slaughter shared the story of how a small rural church became a church of thousands with a global vision and mission. He shared the scars and wounds that come from standing up time after time to share a vision that some rejected. He talked of the very hard work associated with turning an inward church outward. As he shared, he became more and more animated before finally leaving his stool to stand and address this gathering of young pastors. He said, "The gospel is not good news unless it is good news to the poor!"

Those who truly understand the Jesus mission understand that we do not bring good news if it is not good news to the poor. Our vision is not all that compelling if it does not connect with Christ's vision. And, yes, strangely the church still today will offer opposition at times to those who stand up for the poor, the imprisoned, the blind, and the oppressed. But we stand up anyway, because the gospel loses its heartbeat when those Jesus came to save are ignored.

The challenge that New Adapters face today is a church that has turned inward. It is a church that has not loved its neighbors and has not heard the cry of the needy. This challenge, I believe, is our greatest opportunity, because when we connect to the stated vision of Jesus, the church is unleashed. Perhaps better than saying the church is unleashed, the power of God is unleashed on a world that desperately needs the power of God. To do this we must move from inward-focused ministries and simply having "missions" and "outreach" as subsections to a church that sees all of its ministries as focusing on the poor, which includes everyone.

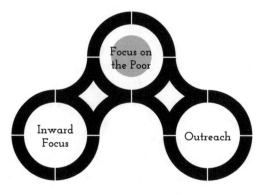

Who Are the Poor?

There are, of course, many ways to be poor. Physically, emotionally, spiritually, financially. Every community is filled with the poor, and every church is called to the poor. An emphasis on and a return to this core vision of Jesus's ministry will be key to the survival of the church. Remember, I am not worried about the church dying. But the churches that ignore the poor around them will die. Many United Methodist churches are in survival mode. It is in these times that we will be tempted to look only to our own needs and subsistence. Our churches will shrivel when we only take care of our own needs. Amazingly, though, when we have the courage to stretch and reach out, the fire of life in the belly of the church begins to grow and grow and grow. This fire is the Holy Spirit, which was given to the first followers of Jesus, which empowered them to leave their locked room hideout and led them to set the world on fire with the message of a God who cares desperately about the poor, oppressed, and imprisoned.

Though it is sad to admit, a key adaption for the church today will be a return to bringing good news to the poor (and we are all poor). It will mean admitting that we have unintentionally turned inward as we have sought to protect our assets. New Adapters will take the assets that we have and realign them to bring good news to the poor. In so doing our goals of survival and subsistence will be met.

So, we must ask, "*Who are the poor to whom my church is called?*"

The book of Acts gives us direction for where we should turn as we consider this question. As Jesus is preparing the disciples for the Holy Spirit's arrival at Pentecost, he says, "*It isn't for you to know the times or seasons that the Father has set by his own authority. Rather, you will receive power when the Holy Spirit has come upon you, and you will be my witnesses in Jerusalem, in all Judea and Samaria, and to the end of the earth*" (Acts 1:7-8). Amazingly, Jesus gives response to the three temptations that he faced in the wilderness and that he knows his followers will face when they set out to fulfill his vision. To the temptation of provision, Jesus says that God will provide a power that will be all we need for the journey. The Holy Spirit becomes our constant reminder and provider on the journey, just like the manna in the desert that our ancestors ate. To the temptation of fame and power, Jesus simply reminds us that timing and results rest on God's authority, not our own. And to the temptation of making a show of God's power, Jesus calls us witnesses who testify to what God has and can do. There shall never be the illusion that we do this on our own; we simply point to our great God.

And Jesus tells us where to find the poor to whom we are called.

They are in Jerusalem. They are in our city. They are in our neighborhoods. They are in our church already. They are outside on the sidewalk.

They are in Judea. They are in the areas surrounding us. They are close by. They are within driving distance. They are among our people.

They are in Samaria. They don't look like us. Their skin is a different color. They worship differently from us. We don't agree on everything. They have hurt us in the past.

They are in the ends of the earth. They are far away. They speak a different language. We will have to travel to see them. Some will be sent there to live.

If it sounds overwhelming to be a church that reaches Jerusalem, Judea, Samaria, and the ends of the earth, just relax. This isn't about us. It's about what the Holy Spirit of God can do when it empowers God's people. And don't worry, your church won't be called to change the whole world alone; there are a bunch of us who are in on this.

New Adapters must first consider the following question: **Who are the poor in my community?** Who are the poor in my Jerusalem? There will be plenty of people who will ask, sometimes with a critical spirit, why we are going halfway around the world when there is so much need here. They are right! There is always so much need here. That means nothing to me about who should be ignored somewhere else, but the place to start is in our neighborhood. Enlist those folks who criticize global missions to help you think about what poor means in your community (then later invite them on an overseas mission trip). Some of the poor, oppressed, and imprisoned will be easy to see. They are sleeping on the street corner; they are in the local jail. Others will be harder to see, but you know them. At Providence Church it was learning about hundreds of homeless students in our community who have no permanent residence and who bounce around from one couch to another, from one backseat to another. It broke our hearts. A task force was created involving school officials, guidance counselors, and other churches whose hearts broke over this need. Ministries were created, and we still ask the Holy Spirit to empower us to love and care for these children. During the 2008 recession, the pastor of a small church in our community identified dozens and dozens of families living in a local RV campground. In our own somewhat affluent community there was a community of people living in tents and lean-tos. Right under our noses, Pastor Larry opened our eyes to a place of need that we now resource with food, worship, and assistance. But the poor in our community are also the depressed, the ones for whom the American Dream has become a nightmare, and the lonely. How will we reach them?

We then ask: **Who are the poor in my Judea?** While there is great need right outside of our doors, God also calls us to consider those in our area who are facing need. I am called to a suburban community. I love it and there are plenty of poor folks spiritually and physically right here in Mt. Juliet. I count myself among them. But within a twenty-minute drive of my front door there is another type of poverty not as apparent in my community. In an area of East Nashville, drug use, prostitution, and hunger are front and center on the street corners. Recently God called us there too. We learned of a young man named Nate who had moved from a farm in Alabama with his wife to love the people who live near the corner of Trinity Lane and Dickerson Pike. Nate, with his *Duck Dynasty* beard in full glory, rides his bike to Trinity United Methodist Church every day, where he opens the doors, literally, to the neighborhood. Trinity UMC was a strong church in the 1940s and '50s, but for years now has been home to only a couple dozen members. While the neighborhood has changed drastically, the worship service inside Trinity has remained the same. Nate helped to start a monthlong summer camp for the children of Trinity. Suddenly this vacant church building was filled with noise, messes, and the Holy Spirit. I attended the camp, and my daughters came with me. We fell in love with the neighborhood as our hearts broke for those in our Judea and as we saw our own poverty hidden in our hearts by the veil of suburbia. Now our church has partnered with the Trinity Community Ministry. We will join with Nate and continue to build a new faith community that will reach out to the poor of East Nashville. **Where is God calling you that is within driving distance of your front door?**

Who are the poor in my Samaria? When Jesus called his followers to be witnesses in Samaria, he was asking them to break a lot of rules, ones he had already broken himself. When Jesus spoke to the Samaritan woman at the well, he broke a number of societal and religious norms. Jesus didn't let differences in religious custom or even centuries of prejudice stop him from sharing living water with her. He instituted at that time that all of his followers would be open to ignoring rules that got in the way of sharing God's love. So bringing good news to the poor is not just about reaching those in our neighborhood who look like us, think like us, and worship like us. It's bigger than that.

A few years back, someone in our church sent me an e-mail. That's usually how it starts. Her heart was broken after watching a news feature on Native American children in Oklahoma. The segment shared that many of these children in our country live in third-world conditions. Addiction is rampant, school drop-out is the norm, poverty abounds. We learned of a community center/church in Clinton, Oklahoma, that had a beautiful ministry with the children of the Cheyenne and Arapahoe tribes. We asked if we could join them. With their yes, our church responded with a large financial gift, and a bunch of us loaded up and went for our first visit. We have since made many return trips, and some of them have visited us. People from our church go on vacation to spend time with our friends in Clinton. We are in relationship as we learn and heal together. You see, what we learned is that we were breaking a bunch of rules. I learned this as I sat as a delegate to the 2012 General Conference of The United Methodist Church. There at a service of repentance, Dr. George Tinker spoke about the unwritten history of the atrocities against his people, Native Americans. He said what we had been taught in school was not the full story. He then shared about the missionaries who did stay and defend the Native Americans when President Jackson ordered the death march to Oklahoma now known as the Trail of Tears. A bit of pride began to swell up in me. "At least some stood up for what is right!" Then he said the missionaries stayed with the Native Americans until the Tennessee Annual Conference of The Methodist Church ordered that the missionaries come home. There would be great land and financial gains for the parishioners of the Tennessee Conference if the Native Americans were forced to leave. The missionaries left and the indigenous people of Tennessee were pulled out of their home. It is hard to describe the emotion, the physical reaction, I had when he spoke those words. I was sitting in the Tennessee Conference section, as a Tennessee Conference delegate, with Tennessee Conference on my name tag. I felt like a spotlight was on me. I began to sweat. Then, I began to cry. I felt so sorry for my heritage. Who could I apologize to? What would it mean if I did? What weight would it carry? I wanted to run to the Native Americans who had gathered in the gallery that night and beg them for forgiveness.

Dr. Tinker said that we are far past the point of apology. And, he said, we are nowhere near reconciliation. His remarks were pointed but full of compassion and grace as he said we must begin the work of repentance together. He did some etymological and exegetical work on the word *repentance* in the Greek and Hebrew scriptures. It was information I had heard before, but it sounded new in that setting. He said that the word in the Greek is a present imperative word implying that we are not to repent now but to repent continually. He also said it is not an individual work, but one done in community. He said in the South we might say, "Y'all repent continually."

I understood. And I felt poor. Really poor. And then my poverty was overwhelmed with a sense of gratefulness for a church that gives me opportunity to repent and be in relationship. Our relationship with the Clinton Indian Methodist Church and Community Center has changed our hearts, and we pray it is changing even more than that.

When Jesus invited his followers to be in ministry with Samaria, he was saying the ones we have hurt, the ones we have disagreed with for centuries, are a part of this call as well. Who are the poor in your Samaria?

Who are the poor in the ends of the earth? In light of the overwhelming scope of the need in the world, New Adapters are attentive to where God has called them and open to how God is calling them to connect. As we have already heard from Mike, the local church in America has a responsibility to the world. But it may be easy to think of the Ginghamsburg example as something that only megachurches can do. Nope. New Adapter Matt Miofsky has taught me how a church of any size can be involved locally and globally. Matt founded The Gathering, a United Methodist church, in St. Louis in

2006. Like many church planters in their first year, Matt and The Gathering found themselves focusing much of their attention, energy, and money on themselves. It is difficult for a new church to become self-sustainable, and things that come naturally for an established church, like the weekly rhythm of planning and leading worship, are big tasks. About eight months in, Matt noticed that much of the focus was inward, and he knew that something had to change. These initial months would be critical for The Gathering in determining the DNA of their church. It would never be convenient to serve those in need. It would never be easy financially. It was eight months in when The Gathering decided to fully fund an emergency daycare for low-income families at a local ministry. It would cost $30,000. Matt stood before his infant congregation that was barely paying their own bills and asked them if they would sacrifice so that these families could have this important service. It would cost them nearly 20 percent of their annual budget. If it jeopardized their own growth, they were willing. They knew the decision would determine the future of their new church. In five weeks, $30,000 was raised and the DNA of The Gathering was set. It also led to greater generosity and growth in their own church.

A few years passed, though, and in a church survey that simply asked, "What do you think of when you think of The Gathering?" Matt noticed an interesting omission from the answers. No one said that they thought of a church that serves the poor when thinking of The Gathering. The vision had leaked as it often does, and the leadership of The Gathering resolved to reestablish themselves as a church that brings good news to the poor. This time to the ends of the earth. During Advent Matt preached about the incarnation and how it shone light on a people in a place that was far away from the center of power. The Gathering determined to help bring safe water to the United Methodist churches that their conference is partnered with in Mozambique. (It's a long way from St. Louis to Mozambique!) They have now built twenty-six wells and have more in progress. But it hasn't just been about sending money or building wells. The Gathering has built and maintained relationships with the people of Mozambique. Teams from The Gathering have traveled there, and Mozambique pastors have traveled to St. Louis! They even have a Mozambican pastor share the prayer in their worship service. They have iPhones in Mozambique too!

On a recent trip to Mozambique, Matt arrived in a remote area after hours on the road to see a village in need of safe drinking water. When he arrived, he saw a pastor standing nearby holding a water bottle with The Gathering's logo on it. Matt approached him and asked about the bottle. The pastor shared with Matt about a church in St. Louis that cares about them, digging wells and building relationships. Matt was moved and humbled to hear someone share about his church and, more importantly, the love of God through his church in a place that to them was at the ends of the earth. Now it didn't feel that far away.

New Adapters are looking for ways to connect their people with the heart of the gospel, which is good news to the poor. When we do not, when we stay mired in inward conversation and patterns of self-service, we cheat our people. New Adapters understand outreach as more than a missions budget; it is the heartbeat of the church.

One thing Nate Paulk and the Trinity Community Ministry have taught me about ministry to the poor is that, moving forward, it must be ministry *with* the poor. Bringing good news to the poor means seeing our own poverty and being in ministry together. On Tuesday nights in an old church on one of the worst street corners in Nashville, there is a community meal. Tables set with real dishes and silverware are filled as people come to eat together. There is no line through which the poor walk, being served from those who have driven in from suburbs. We eat and talk and pray together. We need each other.

This will be another critical adaptation for the inward-facing church to make. Many churches have Wednesday night fellowship meals for members of the church. Many churches also engage in feeding ministries, a food pantry, a soup line, and so on. This was the model before; the adaptation is when these feeding opportunities are integrated in a way where all of us poor people eat together.

A Conversation with Adam and Mike

Adam: The Church of the Resurrection was started in a relatively affluent community, and very early on we made the decision to give the first 25 percent of our offerings away to people outside the walls of the church. Then, over time, as our sense of calling grew, we developed a membership expectation so that everyone who joins the church is asked to be engaged in ministry with the poor or those who are in need in some other way. Nonreligious people are not really sure that they need Jesus. They are not sure they want to read the Bible. But an increasing number of them are really sure they want to make a difference in the world. We believe the church is God's instrument to do that. And so we found that people really noticed and were intrigued when they encountered a church that genuinely cares about people in need, that reaches out to help others and to offer good in the community. And we found that when people engaged with others, they started to grow in their faith. And soon they were feeling energized in their spiritual life, which is exactly what you'd expect when you read the scriptures. It grew from there.

Our theme right now is to turn the church inside out. We are going to send people out to make as many touches as we can. To seek justice and do loving kindness and show compassion for people, and then see what happens as a result. Our people get excited about that. Our faith is more than just me and Jesus. It is Jesus empowering me to go work for his kingdom in the world. That is what a holistic, missional Christianity looks like.

Mike: And what's so important is how this reframes the way people are used to thinking about mission or evangelism. In so many churches, what they call missions or working with the poor is simply donating. As leaders we can reframe our people's hearts and minds when we create exposure for them, when we create partnerships for them in the community, when we get our people out of the four walls of the church. We have to put them in places where they develop relationships with people who are outside their normal experience.

We have to continually build relationships with people who are *not* in the church, those who are in need out in the community, in the world. Leaders have to remember—and teach others—that it's about building relationships with people we otherwise would never meet. Because Jesus works through us when it becomes real for us, because we are in relationship with someone. "I've come to proclaim good news to the poor." That changes hearts. And that's where real conversion takes place.

Adam: This is part of why I became a United Methodist. I found Christ in a Pentecostal church. The mission there was all about telling people about Jesus. If there was someone in need in the church, of course you would help them, because they were part of your church family. But there was never a charge to go out and serve the poor or be engaged in social justice activities. In college I joined The United Methodist Church, and part of what drew me to the denomination was the emphasis on the social gospel. There was a balance between the evangelical gospel and social gospel. Personal holiness, but also a way of living out your faith in the world. That was so captivating for me. When we started Resurrection, it was clear that this was who we were supposed to be. And it was who the early Methodists were. John Wesley and his band of peers at Oxford, poor college students, pooled their resources to hire a tutor to work with children in the streets. And then they'd go into the prisons and into the Kingswood school, and all the rest.

When you stop and think about it, you realize that so much of what Mike and I have tried to lead in our churches is the same stuff that early Methodists did. Their good work led people to pay attention to the words they were saying, to the gospel message they were sharing. So much of what we have done is not really new but is a reclaiming of Methodism in its best expression, as Christians who *demonstrate* this gospel with our lives.

Mike: *Feeling* with people—having compassion, empathy—this is important, too. If as a pastor, you ever lose sight of the one, if you are not losing sleep over the one, then get out of ministry. Do something else. Never lose sight of the one.

Adam: Bishop Handy assigned me in 1990 to start Resurrection. I had told him I'd be willing to go into the inner city, to turn around a dying church in the inner city or start a church out in the community where I'd grown up. And he was this great African American bishop from Louisiana with this deep God-sounding voice, and I'll never forget what he said to me when he assigned me to start our church. He said, "Just remember, those rich people out in the suburbs are poor, too." And he was right. They were poor and broken, too. That is a mission field. And he told me that if we could help turn them around, help them to find hope and healing, they could help to change the world. So it's an interesting dynamic. You clearly see that as a pastor, wherever you are. You see people in their brokenness and you see all their stuff. A lot of people who seem to be wealthy are really two paychecks from being bankrupt.

Chapter Three

NEW SPACES
FOR NEW PEOPLE

There was a time when the people would just come. It was before my time, but not much before. The decades after World War II presented a cultural landscape where the nation centered on the family unit and the American Dream. A part of that pursuit included a connection to the local church. As new suburban communities began to bloom, denominations made sure they had a plot of land and a young pastor to begin constructing a building, then a church. It worked. In a time of strong denominational connection the Methodists moving out of the urban areas looked for a Methodist church, the Baptists a Baptist church, the Episcopalians a Episcopal parish, and so on. Likewise, when a Lutheran moved from Minnesota to Atlanta, the Lutheran sought out a Lutheran church. There were no church shoppers. In a time of great belonging, people knew which tribe they belonged to and went there to worship. This is a generalization to be sure, but one from which a strong conception of church growth and church planting grew out. It has been hard to shake.

There was a slight shift as denominational ties became less and less important and nondenominational churches became more and more prominent. One key identifier of this shift was a focus on programming. Churches began to grow their staffs and offer dynamic, age-appropriate programming for children, youth, and adults. And then programming for toddlers, preteens, young adults, young at heart, and any other age group they could think of. It worked. Families sought out churches with the best programming, and if a Methodist family was not finding their needs met in their local church, they would consider checking out the Baptist church across the street if their kids liked the youth group.

It was a shift, but the basic understanding was still the same. "Here is the church; here is the steeple; open the doors, and see all the people." Or said another way, *Open the doors and the people will come.* They will come if they are a part of our tribe, and then they will come if we offer the programming that fits their family unit.

And then something happened. They stopped coming. It seemed sudden to those of us in the church, but a careful examination of the data shows us that they started to stop coming around forty years ago. We just didn't really notice. We were busy building buildings and programs. But it has caught up with us and there is a need once again for some faithful in the church to listen and learn from our culture and adapt the church to the change in paradigm. This one, though, will not be a slight shift. A slight shift is needed when people stop coming for denominational reasons and start coming for programmatic ones. We made that one on the fly. A major adaptation is needed to reach people who have stopped feeling the need to come. Almost everything will have to change. When worship, children's ministry, youth ministry, and adult discipleship are all built around knowing what to do with the people when they get in the building, we can't make incremental change here. An adaptive change is required. And it goes deeper than the local church. Our larger denominational structures of programming and oversight, our alignment of resources, our theological education, our publishing houses—it all has to change.

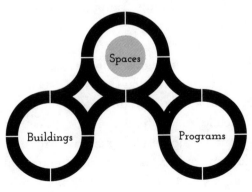

We have to focus on reaching new people. This doesn't mean the people we already have are of less importance. It doesn't mean we have kicked discipleship to the curb. It only acknowledges that a part of this Jesus movement that was kicked into gear at Pentecost has always had a central focus on reaching new people and a core result of new people being reached. (See: three thousand were added unto their number at Pentecost.)

New Spaces for New People Doesn't Always Mean Physical Spaces

One part of this change in thinking about the spaces where people connect with Christ has been seen in a significant change in church planting. Church planting has recently been forced to focus far less on physical buildings and more on building communities of people. For instance, when I was sent to start a new church in a new area, I was given no funds for physical buildings or instruction on where to meet. I was commissioned to reach people. This was scary at first, as someone who grew out of the model of church happening in a building. I soon realized it was a gift.

On the weekend of my first Easter as a church planter in Mt. Juliet, I made the drive from my house to a local city park. It was Saturday and I noticed church after church hosting their annual Easter egg hunts. The parking lots were packed and children filled church lawns covered in pastel-covered eggs. A part of me longed to join them. I had just left a wonderful church where I had served for eight and a half years. I remembered the joyous occasion of taking my own children to the church Easter egg hunt. It was a familiar place with familiar friends. This year, however, I was driving to the city park for an event hosted by our community center called Spring Jam. It was an event for children and families with games, activities, and, of course, an Easter egg hunt. The Spring Jam was sponsored by the city and local businesses. Our new church, which had yet to have its first worship service, was one of the sponsoring entities, and we had a booth with face painting, balloons, and candy.

Over five thousand people attended the Spring Jam that day.

Presumably these were people who did not have a church Easter egg hunt of their own to attend. We shook their hands, painted their kids' faces, and invited them to Providence Church. We left the Spring Jam that day and headed to a local apartment complex where we hosted, on their grounds, a similar Easter celebration with games and activities for the fifty or so children who lived there.

We didn't go out into the community because we understood the paradigm shift that had occurred in the American church over the last fifty years. We didn't do it because we believed there to be anything wrong with events on the church grounds. We did it because we had to do it. We had no land or church building to host our own event, and for that matter, not many children of our own. So we joined with our community and went into the community to encounter people for Christ. We pledged that day, though, to be a church that would not be bound by the walls of a building (again, it was easy for us because we had no building!), a church that would be committed to creating new places for new people and that would start by going to the people.

In a time when those who don't already come to church won't just come to church on their own, we have to be creative in the ways we go to them. It does not mean an abandonment of church buildings or that we should not build new buildings (though perhaps we should build less). It does mean that the buildings are used and seen in different ways than they were before and that we must be committed to our communities in ways we weren't before.

As discussed in chapter 1, we begin by listening to and learning from our communities (even if we have lived there a long time!). Next we commit or recommit ourselves to the people outside the walls of our church. To reach new people, we have to have a visible presence in our community. Look for ways to engage the community where church members and attendees get the opportunity to live their faith by serving others. There are many ways to leverage the land and building you have to serve the community, but for a couple of events a year, I suggest pretending like you don't have those things. *How would you reach out and encounter new people if you did not have a building or land?*

Often the only events churches hold for their communities are fundraisers for things such as building a new playground or sending the youth to camp. While these are worthy ventures (and often necessary because building debt has restricted funds to ministry areas), consider what message your fund-raisers send to those outside of the church: "Come help us do something for us." Instead, do things for the community that are not fund-raisers but instead require your funds, your energy, and your prayers.

On the first day of summer in our first year as a church, we had a cookout with free food and snow cones for a local trailer park. On Armed Forces Day our community invited all military families and veterans to an event. We were there with a prayer wall on which people could write the names of those close to their hearts who have served or were currently serving in the military. The next day in worship we carried the prayer wall into our sanctuary (a movie theater at the time) and prayed for those on the wall. We partnered with a public school to build a Math Garden on their campus to assist in teaching basic math skills to children. On the Fourth of July we co-sponsored a fireworks display at a local shopping mall.

You may ask, "What do these events have to do with the good news of Jesus Christ?" They are ways that we can go into our community, walk the streets as Jesus did, and become acquainted with our mission field. We often see needs that we didn't know existed. We are able to invite others to join us in worship. How can we share the gospel if we never encounter those in need of the gospel? How can we create new opportunities for new people if we don't know who they are? The new spaces for new people are the spaces in the community where the people already are.

Find out what existing community events you can join in on. You may be surprised how willing community organizers are to work with a church on these events. You will establish relationships that will be of value for years to come. If your community does not offer such events, maybe your church should be the one to plan them. Be creative and have fun doing things that your church can uniquely do and offer to others! These events will not always equate to new people in your church, but they will create a culture within your church that you are open to new people, and they will create a reputation in your community that you are outward focused, which will lead to new people in your church. *What spaces outside of your church building are available for you to reach new people?*

So after you have engaged your community, you can then consider what people will experience when they come into the places in your church you already have available for them. Some of these spaces will need to change. In other words, some of your existing spaces (ministries, worship services, physical spaces) will need to become new places.

When Adam Weber received his degree in business he envisioned a career in marketing. He did not envision that he would be the pastor of one of the fastest-growing churches in the nation. And nobody envisioned that one of the fastest-growing churches in the nation would be in Sioux Falls, South Dakota. But when Adam was a young man, Jesus captured his heart and gave him a crazy desire to reach the next person and the next person and the next person for Christ. In July 2007, Adam started Embrace Church in Sioux Falls, where it continues to thrive today.

It is my opinion that Adam is using his marketing degree well as I consider him one of the best at getting the message of Jesus out to people who didn't even know they wanted Jesus. I think that is a pretty good definition of a marketer. He does it in an authentic and careful way, but he is unashamed in his desire to connect other people to Jesus. One of the ways Embrace does this is through the creative use of their space. They have been very intentional in remodeling the old Lutheran church that they first leased and have now bought. The space feels like the kind of place you want to come into. It is comfortable and attractive. It is the kind of place you would invite your friends. It doesn't feel weird. It doesn't say, "We don't care about our building." Instead, it says, "We were hoping you would come." It is not uncommon for Embrace to have movie nights or parties at their campuses. They attract people and then invite those people to connect in worship, small groups, or serving. They have a lot of baptisms. A lot. They have created a new place for new people by re-envisioning an existing church building. It was originally designed as a space for a church, but Adam's team has adapted it into a space that will welcome new people today.

Scott Chrostek was an economics major and was already working at a brokerage firm by the time he was eighteen. He envisioned himself in the investment field for many years to come. Then he felt God calling him to go into urban areas and invest in places and people that the church had been ignoring for a long time. In 2009 he became an urban missionary to downtown Kansas City as a part of a new campus for Church of the Resurrection. Scott felt called to new people. His experience in making cold calls in the business world gave him comfort in seeking to make friends out of strangers and invite them to a new expression of church. Each day he put thirty-five pennies in his right pocket. Each time he met and had a conversation with a new person he moved one penny from the right to the left pocket. He didn't go home until he had thirty-five pennies jingling together in the left side. Resurrection Downtown had their first worship service fifty-three days after Scott arrived in Kansas City. Sixty-eight people accepted Scott's invitation and were among those who gathered for the first worship service. The second worship service saw 113 people who started out as pennies in Scott's pocket. The third service had 140.

The space that they met in was an old United Methodist church in downtown Kansas City. They met on Sunday nights, as there was still a worshipping congregation there on Sunday mornings. It was an old space being used for new people. After several months there, Scott learned of a bar and concert venue that the owner was thinking of selling. He learned this because he had made a relationship with the owner. The purpose of Resurrection is to see nonreligious and nominally religious people become committed followers of Christ. The bar was already a hub for nonreligious and nominally religious people. Scott decided that this would become the new home of Resurrection Downtown. They would build upon the best features of this venue and adapt this community center of sorts into a Christian community center. They used the old concert stage as their chancel. They kept the lighting and sound system. They even kept a stencil of a guitar player that used to be behind the bar. Before the venue was a bar and concert space, it was a car dealership. If you walk into the lobby of Resurrection Downtown today you step onto the original tile showroom floor that had been buried under three feet of concrete.

A building that had once been a car dealership and bar now houses a growing, dynamic church where new people are connecting with Christ. It is surrounded by a strip club, a tattoo parlor, and half a dozen other bars. Scott considers himself in the right spot, and I agree. They have used this space in the same way you can use yours. Allow it to tell the story of the people who have come before while being mindful of the people who will come today.

We must be careful not to simply "program" or offer new events, worship services, and so forth just to do something. We should use what we have learned from listening to our community and from our active engagement with the community to inform what we do and when we do it.

Keep in mind that some of this active engagement is done simply by living in and taking part in the community. New Adapter Mark Sheets, pastor of Good Shepherd, a multisite church in Kansas City, points out,

> When you're in a public space like a grocery store and you see some-
> one who goes to your church, there's a good chance they may be more
> fully present at the store during the week than they were at church
> on Sunday. In that space, at that time, you have an opportunity! If
> you can connect with them, even in a small way, suddenly that store
> can become church for them. You just can't make all the connections
> you want to make on a Sunday, and people see that. New spaces for
> new people are all around us.

As we listen and learn we become more aware of the needs of the people around us. After a season of listening to and learning from our community, three felt needs became apparent to us at Providence: hope, healing, and wholeness. These words became a part of our vision statement. (*The vision of Providence is to see those who feel disconnected from God and the church find hope, healing, and wholeness in Jesus Christ.*) These three words help us as we determine what we should and shouldn't and what we can and can't do. They inform what kinds of spaces need to be created to meet new people.

After moving into a new neighborhood in the Providence area of our city, my daughters began playing with two neighbor boys, Tyler and Matthew. They quickly struck up a friendship and were continually running back and forth from backyard to backyard. As often happens, Rachel and I would have conversations with Roger and Celeste, the boys' parents, while the kids ran around. They often shared with us the difficulties of parenting a child with autism. Matthew, an intelligent, inquisitive young boy, was on the autism spectrum and rarely slept and needed constant supervision. In one of our conversations, I invited Roger and the family to join us at Providence Church. He graciously declined my offer as they had tried to go to church unsuccessfully on several occasions. They felt the stares of those in worship as Matthew "disrupted" the service, and most times one parent spent time with Matthew in the lobby while the other sat uncomfortably alone in worship. They had been asked to shush their child. They had been asked to leave.

After talking with a woman in our church who had extensive experience with autistic children, I invited Roger again with the promise that we would have assistance for the family. They came into a new space for new people. They became a valued part of our faith community. Several weeks after Matthew's first visit, though, I was visited in my office by Julia. Julia had not grown up in the church and had recently been baptized. She shared with me that she had been volunteering in our children's ministry and had been in Matthew's class. She asked me a question that is still seared in my memory: "What are we going to do about all the other Matthews in our community?"

Over a year later, after many meetings and with the assistance of trained experts and professionals, we launched a ministry to families with children of special needs. Now dozens of Providence members are trained to help provide assistance to families on Sunday mornings so that the children have a meaningful experience and the parents have the opportunity to worship. Hope, healing, and wholeness.

A whole segment of our community is now welcomed to our church. New places for new people is not always about growing large numbers in attendance but about welcoming those who have not found a place yet in the family of God.

What are the felt needs in your community? What words would describe these needs? What spaces can you create for them?

A couple of years ago Roger and Celeste and the boys moved back to their hometown in Connecticut. I had kept in touch and knew that they had sought out a church home when they moved back. Recently Roger called, though, with an excitement I had never heard in his voice. He shared with me how they had just successfully launched a ministry to special-needs children in their community. A new space had been created where more families were finding hope, healing, and wholeness in Jesus Christ.

A Conversation with Adam and Mike

Mike: There was a methodology of "build it and they will come" during the 1980s and '90s. We used to call it the Walmart strategy, where you move into an area and people from all the little towns would come—and it did work that way for a long time. But that methodology has ceased to be effective. Increasingly, especially for the unchurched, people identify more with the communities that they're in. I learned from a Wesley Seminary study that 84 percent of people now live in or around urban areas. In the church growth movement of the '70s and '80s, which I was a part of, huge numbers of people had left the cities and moved to the suburbs. Now it's moving in the reverse. So how do we regroup and reclaim those areas of the city?

I really learned what this looks like from a young mother at Ginghamsburg. The bus line stops five miles from our main campus, where we operate a food pantry. This young mother, with her baby, would ride the bus to the bus stop, and then walk the five miles from the bus stop to get food at our food pantry. Then she would walk back to the bus stop with her baby and the food. So it hit me, we've really got to create faith communities that people can reach on foot, or that are directly on the bus lines in urban areas. That is part of creating new places for new people today. That's what we're doing with Ft. McKinley, The Point, Higher Ground, and others.

Adam: Anytime you start a new worship service you are going to reach new people. It's amazing. At our Blue Springs campus we went from one service to two and immediately our attendance went up by 25 percent. It has to do with starting something new and offering the service at a time when people can come who couldn't come or wouldn't come at the other times. We find that when we start a new service, with a different style, at a different time, there is a different energy. There is often energy to something that is new. Just because it's new. Remember, people like to be pioneers. They say, "I want to be part of that," and then they invite their friends, because suddenly they have some skin in the game, are invested personally, and want to help it succeed. So now they're a part of this new thing that they can talk about with their friends, and pretty soon they're inviting their friends to come and be part of it too. Before, they might not have thought to invite their friends because the worship service wasn't their mission project. We find the same principle at work when we start new campuses. We always need to be starting something new—dreaming it, investigating the possibilities, or launching it. Whether it's a new campus or new service, it ignites a passion in people who then invite others to join them in it.

Mike: We have to be open to exploring different kinds of worship, types that go beyond conventional church, like house or cell churches and café churches. We are thinking about how to do church plants in a bar, for instance. We have to explore new places, the places where people are now. Because those communities are where they find their identity—not inside the walls of the conventional church.

Chapter Four

ADAPTIVE WORSHIP

Twenty centuries in and worship remains central to the life of the church. Though the form of worship has and will continue to change, the need for the people of God to gather in community and worship has not and will not change. Worship remains for most the first experience of church they will have and for many the only experience of the church they may have. The pastor spends much of his or her time thinking about and planning for worship. And whether we say we are missional or outward focused or whatever the buzzword may be, worship remains. And worship remains important. This chapter will examine ways that we should adapt worship to reach people who are not being reached while still connecting with those already in the seats. It assumes the understanding that worship is to honor and praise God while also fulfilling an important function for the believer.

Opening the Closed Loop

If you attend a service at Resurrection or Ginghamsburg on any given weekend you will find multiple expressions of worship in multiple locations. The music will be different in each. One service will feel more formal, another more casual. In some services, worshippers will hold a hymnal; in others they will look at a screen. We all pretty much get this. We have to adapt the way we "do" worship to connect with different types of people and to connect with a changing culture. The adaptation that we often miss, though, is one that is more subtle. If you have been in the church for a while, you will easily miss it. The outsider, though, feels it almost immediately. One thing that Resurrection, Ginghamsburg, and the growing churches of other New Adapters don't miss is the need to continually make worship accessible to those new to the church.

This will be the key worship adaptation needed for most churches. Many churches have brought in screens and bands, and their pastors wear jeans. This means little to nothing if no attention has been given to the environment of exclusivity that exists in many of our worship services. This means we will have to give up some things that feel really comfortable to us because it feels terribly uncomfortable for the newcomer. It doesn't mean the preferences of the faithful will be ignored, but it does mean we will care more about others than ourselves. Jesus taught us this. Jesus modeled this for us. He was constantly looking to the one on the outside of the community, the one that had been pushed to the edges, the one disconnected from God. This means our worship services should always keep these folks in mind as well.

Many churches have what I call a closed loop. We have a way of doing things, a way of talking, and a way of worshipping that doesn't allow for new people to connect. Without even knowing it, we exclude those we truly want to reach.

Let me illustrate how this might look in a local church. A guest arrives at a church that is new to her. She learned of the service times from the website. She is nervous. She almost talked herself out of coming five times on the drive over. But something drew her to worship. She easily finds a parking place but isn't quite clear where to enter the building. She follows another family in a door, and is greeted quickly by someone who hands her a folded piece of paper. She realizes quickly that she is early, really early. Later she will learn that the church had changed service times but neglected to make the change on the website. Everybody else arrives on time. The first thing that happens in worship is the sharing of announcements. A lot of announcements. Sounds like a lot is going on, but it is hard for her to decipher what all the events are. The letters *VBS* mean nothing to her. She wonders why a rummage sale would be so important to a church. The next thing the person speaking (no idea who the person is) does is invite people to stand and "pass the peace." She stands, but doesn't know what to pass. A couple of kind people come and shake her hand, but then move on to someone else. She stands awkwardly as she hears others talking with their friends about the events of last night. They then sing a song. She realizes the numbers in the folded program refer to a number of a song in the book in the pew in front of her. She stands to sing and feels some comfort as she hears the sounds of voices mixing together in song. After the song, another unidentified individual asks for "joys and concerns." People begin sharing requests for prayer. She doesn't know any of the folks being discussed, but everyone else seems to as they nod with knowing looks as each prayer request is lifted up and updated.

I'll stop there. Without knowing it, many of our church worship services have created a closed loop that is very hard to break through. Some persistent ones hang in there and eventually understand the lingo and the patterns. Other more experienced churchgoers get it right away and have no trouble assimilating. But for the church to adapt in a way that leads to life for more people, we must care enough to open the closed loop to let new people in. And this will hurt. It will hurt because things like church announcements, passing the peace, and joys and concerns make the regular church attender, those on the inside of the loop, feel connected and valued.

We must be willing, though, to think about everything we do in worship through the eyes of the newcomer. It may mean giving up the passing of the peace because we realize this is not a time when guests feel more welcomed, but more isolated. It may mean finding other arenas where prayer requests can be shared and actually prayed over. It may mean sharing fewer announcements in worship and spending more time focusing on connecting people to God. In short, opening the closed loop demands **intentionality**. A worship service that lacks intentionality will exclude people who are not accustomed to our ways. And Jesus cares about those people. A lot.

New Adapters are intentional, and **intentionality starts in preparation**. Preparation for worship should take into mind what we have heard and learned from our community. You may determine that organ and choral music is the best way to reach your community. You may not. But those learnings lead to intentional decisions about what you do in worship. The question of intention is "why?" Why are we singing this song? Why are we having a children's moment? Why are we making seven announcements? These questions are tested against the vision that was discerned in listening to God and learning from your community. Having a clear vision of the purpose of your church allows you to adapt in intentional ways that will open the closed loop of worship. People who come for the first time and those who are returning for their one-hundredth time appreciate the intentional decisions made to include everyone in the worship of God. They may never notice it or thank you for your intentionality, but they will feel it…and they will return.

One quick distinction so there isn't confusion as we proceed. **Intentionality doesn't mean excellence or perfection.** Many of us strive toward excellence in worship. At Providence, we rarely achieve it, but we strive for it. Intentionality, though, doesn't mean excellence will always be achieved, and intentionality is more important than excellence. Being intentional doesn't mean being spotless or flashy. At Ginghamsburg, Mike has seen how an emphasis on excellence has shifted to a focus on including more people. Less excellent, but more inclusive. Your band will be more technically excellent if every member is paid. I assure you of that. However, you may find as you focus on reaching those who feel disconnected from God, that church becomes less excellent and messier. That's okay. Don't mishear me. I think worship music should be good, hopefully really good. Sloppy music or bad preaching will be as effective at keeping guests from returning as anything. Just don't confuse intentionality with excellence. They are different, and intentionality is more important.

Intentionality is the first step in opening worship up to new people, and it leads to a key adaptation in how we speak. One of the great adaptations needed today in the church regards language. This shouldn't surprise us. On the Day of Pentecost, the day we recognize as the birth of the church, there were a lot of crazy things that happened. One thing that happened on the church's first day was that people spoke in different languages. As the wild Holy Spirit outpouring gathered a crowd, people from all over the world could hear the followers of Jesus speaking in their native tongue. I often wonder why we in the church seem to speak a different language from our communities, when the church was initially known for adapting language so all people could understand. I'm not suggesting that the terms *narthex* and *fellowship hall* should be discarded (okay, maybe I am), but I am suggesting that we think about what we say. To open the closed loop and invite others into our worship experiences, **we must be intentional about how**

we talk. I learned from Adam Hamilton early on that a simple self-introduction before you speak in worship goes a long way in making people feel welcome. Sure, most people in attendance at Providence know who I am. But since we have multiple guests each Sunday, I introduce myself before I speak, as do others who speak in worship. It's also important to unpack or translate churchy language into the common vernacular. We can't assume anymore that we can just say "the Trinity" or other helpful descriptive theological terms and expect that people know what we are talking about. When we use insider language it keeps the loop closed tightly. This doesn't mean that we discard the terms. There are some great church words that we want people to know. It just means we can't expect that they already know them. We should care enough to translate, and I have found that even our regular attenders appreciate the reminders. Notice that this in no way compromises what we say. At Pentecost, Peter explained the strange outburst of different languages to the people gathered as something that the Holy Spirit had done. Then, with the language barriers down, he took the opportunity to share about who Jesus was and what he could do for each person there. Thousands were saved. Their "worship service" that day was unlike any other before. The location, the outward expressions, the languages spoken were all different. And yet, the message of God's redeeming love through Jesus Christ was communicated and lives were changed. In many cases, the location, the way it looks, and the way we speak in worship should be adapted. The message of God's redeeming love through Jesus Christ is unchanging and still is the only thing that changes lives. Pentecost was about inviting the whole world into the God story. Think about what you say in worship and encourage those others who are speaking to think about it too. It is a simple way to open big doors to invite others in.

New Ways of Worship Look Old

This connects with another finding of New Adapters today: new ways of worship look old. Robert Wuthnow, professor of sociology and director of the Center for the Study of Religion at Princeton University, has done extensive research on young adults and American religion. In his book *After the Baby Boomers*, he writes that young adults "think church services should feel like church. They say the so-called seeker services that were geared toward people who disliked church are now passé" ([Princeton, NJ: Princeton University Press, 2007], 223-24). In a major research project on the uses of music and arts in congregations, Wuthnow observed that young adults were often as interested in preserving traditional worship as they were in changing it. Many New Adapters are finding that new ways of worship look familiar; they look old. While baby boomers still have a strong connection to so-called contemporary worship, many others are connecting with worship through traditional elements. This does not mean we pump up the organ music and watch the hipsters line up to get in the church doors. It does mean, though, that we can't throw a band together, put on blue jeans, and expect church growth (anymore). Sad, I know. It means we must be intentional in creating worship experiences that incorporate the ancient and modern. It means authenticity and honesty are more important than worship style.

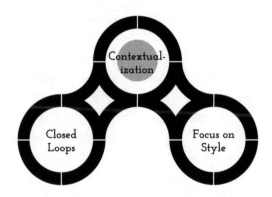

Contextualization of Worship

Matt Miofsky and The Gathering in St. Louis are leaders in adapting worship to fit context. They have also seen that many new forms of worship still look old. In their visioning stage, they didn't ask people in St. Louis what they don't like about church, but instead they asked, "What does church look like?" They learned that many of their assumptions were incorrect. In a heavily Catholic city, Matt found that many people expected ritual and tradition in worship. They weren't interested in a church that pretended it had no past. Their music tastes were eclectic, and aesthetics were important to most people. Holy spaces matter. If you worship at The Gathering you will find a creative worship experience that is unique and beautiful. You will also find a church that has incorporated ancient elements of worship to reach new people for Christ. They seek to have worship that is historically rooted and innovatively practiced. I agree with Matt when he says, "It is arrogant to think that the brothers and sisters who came before us don't have anything to teach us." So when they think about, for instance, responses to the Word of God, they ask, "What are responses that are historically rooted?" Healing, offering, communion, and testimony come to mind. Then they ask, "How can we practice this in an innovative way?" Their worship also evolves over time. What they are doing today is not what they did five years ago or even last year. When they began, Matt and the other pastors wore robes and stoles in worship. Today they do not, but perhaps they will again. They are continually listening to their context to determine how to adapt their services. When they started, Matt preached the lectionary; today they preach sermon series while still connecting with many elements of the church year.

In the same way, Olu Brown at Impact (remember, a church that is doing things differently) still regularly incorporates elements of worship that would have been common in the traditional urban African American church. These elements are intentionally included in an innovative way in a nontraditional setting. They speak deeply to those who attend in a way that they can hear.

Matt and The Gathering and Olu and Impact teach us that the doors are wide open for creative expressions of worship that honor our heritage and breathe with new life and imagination.

At Providence we pray the Lord's Prayer, say the liturgy for Holy Communion, and sing hymns. Our music isn't loud, and we don't ask people to stand for forty-minute worship sets. No one would accuse us of having traditional worship. Blended isn't the right word for it either. It is whatever it is. We think it fits our community. It speaks of an eternal God, an ancient faith, and the new life found in both.

So as you are planning new expressions of worship, don't out-cool your community and don't throw something out just because it's old. Think intentionally about what will work in your context. Remember that no one will know your community like you and your people if you have done the necessary discerning work. When you attend a conference and hear the next great idea, it is likely the idea holds merit. It is your job, though, to adapt it to your community. You are the chief interpreter who will translate the message into a language your people can understand.

The Twenty-First-Century Lectionary

A principle form of communication in worship is still the sermon. We still devote a considerable amount of time in the worship service to allow one person to communicate a prepared (hopefully) adaptation from the scriptures (hopefully). For millennia now there has been a structure and calendar for what scriptures will be read and taught in worship. The practice of reading appointed scriptures on given dates goes back to the time of Moses. The annual religious festivals of Passover, Pentecost, and the Feast of Tabernacles were a precursor to the Christian year, Christian calendar, or lectionary that many churches follow today. The liturgical year has been a way for Christians, year by year, to "relive the foundational events of the gospel while continuing in the necessary ordinariness of their work and family" (Gail R. O'Day and Charles Hackett, *Preaching the Revised Common Lectionary: A Guide* [Nashville: Abingdon Press, 2007], 30). The implicit strategy of the liturgical year is "the repetitive reliving of the foundational events of Christianity" (O'Day and Hackett, 30). This re-living in worship is meant to form a way of framing all the events of life so that the worshipper finds connection between the holy story and their own story. There have always been faithful people who choose what scripture we hear each week. They sought to construct a plan so that each year a worshipping congregation could hear the story of God's love, grace, and redemption. Of course, you can't get it all, but with a heart toward communicating what is important to grow as a disciple, a weekly plan for hearing the story was made. Sounds like a great idea. But keep in mind: people made the plan. The lectionary was not zapped down onto tablets from on high. Good, faithful people who held a knowledge of the scriptures and the needs of the people in both hands made a good and faithful plan. The lectionary is a wonderful tool for helping to communicate the gospel to a group of people over a period of time. For many New Adapters, though, the twenty-first-century lectionary is not one sent down from denominational higher-ups but instead one that is developed in the community of faith with the community at large in mind.

(Quick aside: I do not hate or look down on preaching the lectionary. I went to an Episcopal seminary. For three years I was on a lectionary IV. I have seen the lectionary be extremely effective. Again, the lectionary tells the story of Jesus in a carefully planned-out way over the course of the whole year. But God didn't set the lectionary, so I feel fine doing something else.)

The twenty-first-century lectionary, I think, is a carefully planned-out schedule of sermon series that attempts to achieve exactly what the people of God were seeking to do when they set the feast days. We remember the story of God and see ourselves as the continuation of it.

At Providence, over the course of a year (after learning from and listening to our community), we consider the needs of our church and tell the story of Jesus through carefully planned sermon series. We don't miss Advent or Lent (and that Easter thing). We think Pentecost should be lifted up every year. But our folks don't know what Kingdomtide is (I'm not sure I do either) and probably aren't sure what color should be on the altar for each season. If your heart is to continue to reach people in your community who are not already in church, the sermon series is a great way to tell the story of Jesus while hooking people for the first time and creating a reason for them to come back the next week. After listening to the community, sermon series can be created that connect to felt needs in the community that will give some folks the impetus to come to your church for the first time. It almost always also includes a personal invitation, but having a theme that connects with a real need in someone's life is a great tool to connecting them to God's story. In an age where attention spans are short, we can create a church-wide focus for four, six, or eight weeks that helps people hear scripture and connect it to their lives.

As we have listened to our community the same felt needs continually rise to the top as the main things people are facing in their lives. (I have mentioned already we classify those needs into hope, healing, and wholeness. More specifically, this may include things such as: a general anxiety about our crazy world, a desire for healthy relationships, and wondering, "What can I give my life to?") We use these felt needs to inform our preaching. We don't craft every sermon series around what people are feeling. But there are key times in a year when we appeal to those felt needs because we want to reach people who aren't in church. Like the faithful formers of the lectionary, we have things that we believe are important to talk about every year, and we create a rhythm that works for us. For a long time Adam Hamilton and Resurrection have alternated a fishing series (a series meant to hook the newcomer) with a more traditional study that will appeal to the faithful churchgoer.

At Embrace in Sioux Falls, Adam Weber and his team offer a topical fishing-type series in September (back to school) and in January. These are the two times when they have the most first-time guests as people in their community are thinking about forming new habits. They use February or March for stewardship and July or August for reinforcing the vision, and they commonly use the lectionary in other times of the year. Your context will be different. My friend Mike pastors a church in southern Florida that experiences its biggest growth in the winter, when many people come to sunny Florida during the cold months up north.

Crafting a sermon series is an adaptive work in itself. It goes through many stages of revision before it is preached. Here are some steps that can be used in crafting sermon series to fit a rhythm for your church:

Continue listening and learning: As you continue listening to and learning from your community, take notes! A conversation in the community may lead to you noticing a greater felt need for many who live among you.

Schedule time away for planning: You will not be able to craft a sermon series in an intentional way if there is no set-aside time for planning. Adam plans a year in advance. Six months may be more realistic for you and your team. Whatever it is, have a plan and a schedule for when the sermon series are to be at differing levels of readiness.

Get other people's eyes on it: Because this is a sermon series for your particular church and community, don't let the pastor's eyes be the only ones that see it before preaching. Get different eyes on it so different voices can help shape it. Make sure your staff team is a part of this in some way so they can shape their teaching ministries around the series as well.

Get it done ahead of time: Did I already say that? For there to be true connectivity and for other support pieces to be completed on time, you must meet your deadlines.

A Conversation with Mike and Adam

Adam: We are always thinking about the language we use and the way we design worship with this question in mind: If you were here for the very first time how would this feel? So we are asking those kind of questions, making sure that we are thinking about what it's going to take to help someone be drawn in rather than put off. We explain baptism every week. We explain what Communion means every time we receive the Eucharist. We put the words to the Lord's Prayer on the screen. All these things are aimed at helping nonreligious people get it, because so much of church doesn't come naturally to people. We don't use creeds very often, because when we are asking people to recite, "I believe in" whatever, well they don't believe that quite yet, and they are not ready to recite it. So we use those sorts of things sparingly and thoughtfully in our worship services.

Mike: Adam, you're also very personable, which is important. You're there with a few thousand people in the sanctuary, but in a baptism, for instance, there is one couple and their baby in that moment. And it is important to realize that every single person matters to God. And we have to ask, "How does our worship experience express that?"

Chapter Five

CONFLICT AND CRITICISM

You've probably heard someone say it before. It's possible the words may have come out of your mouth. It commonly comes after a long wait or a frustrating experience. It sounds something like this: "I will never ever come back to this establishment!" Or "I will never return to this restaurant for the rest of my life." Or "As long as I'm breathing I will not darken the door of this place again!" A clear-cut proclamation of personal disdain for a place because of a terrible experience and you want to make sure everyone within earshot knows that this is your last time here.

And to the best of my memory I have only done it once. Several years ago, when my Mary was three we went to a pizza eatery that caters to children. They have a lot of video games, loud music, and flashing lights, and as a new parent I had no idea what I was getting myself into. After a couple hours of watching an animatronic mouse sing classic rock; spending more than a reasonable amount of my week's salary on tokens that equated to tickets, which led to prizes that were worth only thirty-five cents; and loading Mary up on sugar to the point of sensory overload, I proclaimed to anyone listening, who at that time was only my three-year-old daughter, "I will never come back to this establishment again! As long as I'm breathing I will not darken the door of this place again!"

Well, you know what happens when you say something like that…a couple months later I was approaching the mall with my family, now with two little girls in tow, pushing them in a double stroller. As we were walking up to the mall entrance the two-toothed mouse logo began calling out to my daughters like a beacon, and they began begging, "Please let us go, please let us go!" Rachel, I guess having forgotten my clear-cut proclamation of personal disdain, said to the girls, "If you girls are good while we shop we will take you to Chuck E. Cheese." (For new parents this is called bargaining.) We hadn't been in the mall fifteen minutes before little Lydia was squirming and whining a bit. I said, "Lydia's out. She's not going." And then to my amazement, for the next hour Mary sat there like a statue. Didn't ask for a Cinnabon, didn't ask for a penny to throw into the fountain, didn't complain. Perfect behavior. When we were getting ready to leave, I gathered them up and said, "Good job, Mary, but we are a team here and if one of us can't go, none of us can go." Rachel stepped in and shot me a look that said, "You're going to Chuck E. Cheese." In fact, she said, "I'm going to shop some more, you take the girls to Chuck E., and I'll meet up with you in a bit."

I'll never forget standing in the Stones River Mall in Murfreesboro, Tennessee, and the feeling of turning that double stroller around to head back to where I said I would never return again.

New Adapters know that God is leading us somewhere. We are on the move. We don't always know where, but we know we have to go. And if there is one thing I can guarantee you, it is this: there will come a time when you are tempted to turn back.

There will come a time when either the doubts in your head or the audible voices in your ears will say, "Let's just go back." And they will be beckoning you back to the place that you said you would never return again.

I heard former dean of Duke Divinity School Greg Jones say, "Every church has a Back to Egypt Committee." He was referring to those who wore Moses down with their complaining and grumbling as they hearkened back to a time in their past. One of the greatest dangers to New Adapters is being worn down by those who call us to go back to where we said we would never return.

You remember Moses. Given a vision by God to save a people. After spending some time listening to God in the wilderness, he went to do what God called him to do. Like Jesus he left his time in the desert with a laser-like focus on setting God's people free. Moses led the people out of slavery, and with the Egyptian army on their heels, this mass of freed slaves came to the edge of the Red Sea. It was a long way around, and they could hear the hooves of the horses of the chariots of Egypt coming to take them out. The people looked at Moses and said, "Moses! Was it because there were no graves in Egypt that you brought us here to die? Wouldn't it have been better to be slaves in Egypt than to be massacred in the desert?" Moses, though, could see the vision so clearly; he could still hear God's words ringing in his ears, and he replied, "Do not be afraid, stand firm, and you will see the deliverance the Lord will bring you today. The Egyptians you see today you will never see again." In other words, God led us here, God will lead us out, and we are never returning to Egypt.

Moses stretched out his staff and the sea split and the people of God walked through.

Can you guess where Moses took the people first? Right back into the wilderness! (Hint: spending time in the wilderness is a part of going where God wants.) Out in the wilderness, the people of God got hungry. They said, "Moses, did you bring us out into the wilderness to starve? Didn't we at least have food in Egypt?" It burned Moses a bit, but he was focused on the vision God had given him. Moses was able to hear God's word of provision, a promise of bread from heaven every day. God gave everything they needed for the journey. God gave food. God gave water. God gave clear direction.

But weeks turned into months and months turned into years. And years is a long time to travel around with no place to call your home. And the people began to complain. They were tired of bread. And one night they were sitting around the campfire and somebody said, "Remember what we had in Egypt? Meat."

Some of them were too young to even remember Egypt, but they had heard the stories.

Another said, "Yeah, we had meat and fish." Another said, "We had onions and garlic."

Someone else remembered, "And cucumbers!" You know it has gotten bad when folks start daydreaming about cucumbers.

And then a voice from the shadows, from the outskirts of the campfire..."Why don't we just go back?" Silence. "Why don't we just go back to Egypt?"

Everyone agreed.

There was a time when Moses would have gathered them together and said, "We've got this!" He would have reminded them of God's promise and God's provision. "We can't give up now!" he would have said. But, Moses was tired. He was angry. And instead of recasting the vision, Moses had a breakdown.

Perhaps for the first time Moses began to listen more to the voice of the Back to Egypt Committee than to the voice of God. And the people of God felt their hearts turning back to the one place they said they would never return.

Back at the mall, I turned the double stroller around and started walking back to Chuck E. Cheese, all the while thinking, *What in the world am I doing?*

Every leader will have to face the Back to Egypt Committee, but some will be able to ignore it. The adaptive leader will not. If you seek to do adaptive work, know that complaints are guaranteed and guaranteed to be loud. It is important not to put earplugs in and ignore them but to recognize their voice. Recognize them for what they are, and like Jesus have a response founded on the word of God that allows you to keep going where God has called you.

There are three things that the Back to Egypt Committee will say to you. Be ready for them.

We won't have all we need.

It was better back in Egypt.

You have to do it on your own.

These are what we call lies. But they will seem like pure truth when they come out of the mouths of the convincing committee on return.

Lie: We won't have all we need.

Truth: If God calls you to something, God will provide all you need.

At every juncture, the people of Israel were given a reminder that the vision God had given them was the truth. God said he would get them out of Egypt, and then did so. God gave food, God gave water, God showed them the way. But weeks on the journey turn into months that turn into years, and the years can make you tired. Fatigue has a way of making you focus on what you don't have instead of what you do have. Frustration makes it easier to see the gaps in what we can do rather than the power of what God can do. Time in the wilderness often leads to a scarcity mentality, where we become fixated on what we lack. It leads to an infiltrating hopelessness that makes us think we were foolish to ever leave the comfortable past behind.

New Adapters, though, will look for the potential in what God can do. They will remember the reality of the past and the reasons that they stepped out into change. They will remind the people of God's faithful provision. In a world that says, "I'll believe it when I see it," the New Adapter holds to the faith of the Red Sea-splitting God who calls us to "believe it until we see it."

Lie: It was better back in Egypt.

Truth: A lifetime of slavery is not better than a season of wandering.

"It was better back in Egypt," the folks around the campfire will say. And strangely, absurdly, that makes sense to people. They were enslaved. They had taskmasters who required of them more than was humanly possible. At one point, their babies were killed. And yet weeks that turn into months that turn into years can make you believe the unthinkable. Someone says, "We had meat back in Egypt." And another, "And cucumbers!" Then all of the sudden we are planning a return trip to the land where we were oppressed!

When put like that it sounds crazy, but take my word for it: there will be times when you are on a long journey, heading toward the vision God has for you, and you will hear that voice. The voice of the Back to Egypt Committee will say that it was better back there. But it wasn't; that is a lie. At my church there are many of us who have given ourselves to Jesus in a way we never have before, many who have given up lives of addiction and harmful relationships. We've seen it. And without fail, only steps into the new journey, we are tempted to go back. But, we have also learned that the journey with God when you're not there yet and the vision is not fulfilled is so much better than that from which God delivered us.

I liken it to hanging out with some of my old buddies. Sometimes we get together and reminisce about the past. We romanticize about it. Remember how great it was back then! And then I remember as we glorify the good ole days how miserable we were. I remember how empty I felt when I went to bed at night. I remember how late nights led to hopeless mornings. I think how glad I am that we have continued on the journey. We have helped each other through lost jobs and divorce and struggles with our children. I don't want to go back; I want to keep going.

The church is moving out of a season of romanticizing a bygone era that upon close examination wasn't really the good ole days. We are moving out of it because the writing is on the wall for our demise if we don't change, but still we can get pretty nostalgic. The New Adapter celebrates the beautiful parts of our past, but keeps the church moving forward. We remember a church that was segregated, that excluded people based on status and gender, a church that turned inward and ignored its neighbors, and the leader says, "We are going somewhere else." The leader hears the inevitable grumbling and pushes on.

DJ Del Rosario, a New Adapter in the Pacific Northwest, has faced his share of grumbling and pushed on. As a solo pastor starting at a small church in rural Washington, he immediately faced institutional racism and a lot of plain old resistance. DJ had a heart for seeing the church meet the needs of the community, but most were content with things staying just the way they were. DJ was not content. After his first sermon an older member of the congregation told him that his preaching "makes me want to throw up." At least they didn't mince words. DJ drew upon a reserve that was not mere determination; he was focused on a vision to reach people with the good news of Jesus Christ. Attacks were not personal; they were just a natural part of doing something courageous. DJ brought rocking chairs into the sanctuary as a way of saying, "We welcome young families." Every Sunday when he arrived, the rocking chairs had been pulled out. Every Sunday he brought them back in. Before long, the rocking chairs were filled with young parents rocking their children while DJ preached his nausea-inducing sermons. The church changed because DJ did not allow the romance of the way things were to cloud his vision of where God was leading them.

DJ is now the pastor of Bothell United Methodist Church. He conducted a community audit that sought to answer the question "How can we help people experience God in a real authentic way?" After reviewing the responses of the audit, DJ knew they must change their worship services. He changed their three identical services into three different experiences that would reach different types of people, and he received some notes. There are always notes. You know the notes. Notes that threatened to withhold money if something wasn't done. Notes that were personal when they shouldn't have been. DJ told me that he kept the notes and later wrote them thank-you notes for expressing their feedback (I love this dude!) but reminded them that the church was committed to going to a different place. DJ said, "It was our journey, our vision, not mine, so I didn't take it personally."

Remember that people will always hearken back to a previous day. If God has called you to take the people somewhere else, then keep pushing.

Lie: You have to do it on your own.
Truth: God will give leaders to share the burden with you.

The third lie, you have to do it on your own, is perhaps the most dangerous. Our next chapter will be devoted to uncovering the truth God gives us when we find ourselves isolated and leading alone.

But before moving on, we must examine an essential ingredient to moving a group of people from the lies of the Back to Egypt Committee to the truths that we believe about following God. The missing ingredient in many leaders: courage.

Most of us can feel the Cowardly Lion's pain when he asks: "What makes a king out of a slave? Courage! What makes the flag on the mast to wave? Courage! What makes the elephant charge his tusk in the misty mist, or the dusky dusk? What makes the muskrat guard his musk? Courage! What makes the sphinx the seventh wonder? Courage! What makes the dawn come up like thunder? Courage! What makes the Hottentot so hot? What puts the 'ape' in apricot? What have they got that I ain't got?" (Noel Langley, Florence Ryerson, and Edgar Allan Woolf, *The Wizard of Oz*, directed by Victor Fleming [1939; Beverly Hills, CA: MGM, 1999], DVD.)

Courage! (Did I really just quote the Cowardly Lion? My movie selection is limited with three daughters.)

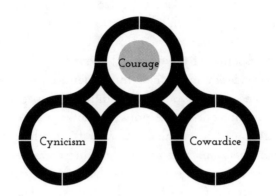

Courage

Hard adaptive work requires courage. And courage is often beat out of us in the early stages of the journey. But, our work is too important to become quivering masses of availability. And courage is not something we muster up. We don't pull our bootstraps up and discover more nerve. We find it in and through our courageous God.

When young Joshua was handed over the reins to the wandering people of God (remember that Moses was denied entry into the promised land because he listened more to the voice of the BTE Committee than to the voice of God), God gave him this word three times: courage.

Be strong and courageous. God's repetitive message to the new leader who would take his people into a new land was courage. I have often wondered why God felt the need to say it three times. My best guess is that it was the most important thing that Joshua needed to hear. He was told some really important things: God will never leave him; obey the law; keep God's word on his lips. But three times, God said to be courageous. It was something God could give, something God could do in Joshua.

In fact, God gives a similar message all throughout the story of God's people. Dozens of times God or someone speaking for God says, "Do not fear." In the scriptures, when we read each Advent about the message of Jesus's arrival in the world, we hear it over and over again. Zechariah, Mary, Joseph, and the shepherds were all told, "Do not be afraid." As we realize that God is going to use us to bring Jesus into our world, our first reaction will be fear.

Take courage. Do not be afraid. The work is too important.

Here are three keys to courageous leadership that I have learned from New Adapters over the years:

Make the hard decisions early. In the beginning stages of starting Providence Church there began talk of making our new ministry a second campus of another church. Multiple campuses are a beautiful model for ministry. There would have been advantages to us doing it. But it wasn't what I felt called to do, and our vision and the vision of the supporting church didn't match. One of my mentors advised me to have hard conversations now to avoid certain misery later. We did. It was painful. I made some people mad. I lost friends that I'd had for years. But I'm convinced that had we not made the hard decision early, it would have cost many months of time and energy. When we lack courage, we often delay decisions that we know should be made now. Be strong and courageous.

Don't avoid conflict. Most of us have an aversion to conflict. It seems natural to want to avoid conflict to some extent. Others of us, though, and many in ministry, exhibit an unhealthy avoidance of disagreement that can lead to huge roadblocks in doing adaptive work in the church. Several years into starting the new church I realized that one of my biggest weaknesses, the avoidance of conflict, had led to a culture of it. One of the things we often forget as leaders is that our strengths and our weaknesses get passed down and through the organizations or teams we lead. In an effort to maintain unity and peace, I had built a system where people didn't know how to have healthy conflict. Because I didn't know how. Well, I think I knew how, but I often lacked the courage to do so. Ironically, though, as conflict avoiders seek to maintain peace and unity, we actually create more tension. Patrick Lencioni writes about this in his book *The Five Dysfunctions of a Team*. He says that when we "do not openly debate and disagree about important ideas, they often turn to back-channel personal attacks, which are far nastier and more harmful than any heated argument over issues" ([San Francisco: Jossey-Bass, 2002], 203). He also notes that "so many people avoid conflict in the name of efficiency" when healthy conflict is actually a time saver. As we take the courage to engage in healthy conflict we are actually more honest and open with our people and can more quickly move toward where God wants us to go.

Remember that criticism is often not about you. Okay, sometimes it's all about you. But more often, criticism is a function of something happening in the critic and has little to do with you. The sooner we begin to see criticism as something less personal and more systematic, the quicker we can resolve problems and avoid the wounds that often go with criticism. In my first appointment as an associate pastor at a large county seat congregation, I was approached by a lady in the narthex (lobby) who had something on her mind. Moments before in worship, upon the suggestion of my senior pastor, I had read from a different version of the Bible than we usually used in that church. To this woman, it was an abomination and she let me have it. She yelled at me and even made personal attacks because I had not used whatever version of the Bible she considered divine. While she was yelling, I heard God speak in my spirit, *Jacob, this is not about you.* It freed me to care for the woman who was upset. It released me from insecurities brought upon by her criticism. It released me from retaliating in an unfaithful way. She finished, and I went to lunch. Now this is, of course, easier said than done. Being accosted for not reading the King James Version of the Bible is different than getting a letter from a church member that calls your integrity into question. I only recommend that you listen for the parts of the criticism that are true, and let the rest fall away. It takes courage to do that. Not to ignore criticism, which is really hard, but to realize it will always be there and *especially* will be there if you are seeking to lead people to a new land. In fact, it is worth asking yourself if you are willing to endure some scrapes and bruises for the cause of the mission. I'm guessing you are.

You have probably heard the quote from Teddy Roosevelt regarding the critic. It bears repeating here.

> It is not the critic who counts; not the man who points out how the strong man stumbles, or where the doer of deeds could have done them better. The credit belongs to the man who is actually in the arena, whose face is marred by dust and sweat and blood; who strives valiantly; who errs, who comes short again and again, because there is no effort without error and shortcoming; but who does actually strive to do the deeds; who knows great enthusiasms, the great devotions; who spends himself in a worthy cause; who at the best knows in the end the triumph of high achievement, and who at the worst, if he fails, at least fails daring greatly, so that his place shall never be with those cold and timid souls who neither know victory nor defeat. ("Citizenship in a Republic" [speech, the Sorbonne, Paris, April 23, 1910])

God is calling you into the arena. God has called you to lead. It will require courage. And what a pity if we let those who criticize keep us from the vision God has for us. We should listen to the comments of others, we should always seek to be self-aware, but we shouldn't let those who have decided to take a different path from us keep us from moving toward the promised land, even if it takes weeks, months, or years. We should be careful whom we listen to and how deeply we listen to them. Dr. Brené Brown, in hearing the Roosevelt quote, said she has decided that "if you are not in the arena with the rest of us,...I'm not interested in your feedback" (*Daring Greatly* [New York: Gotham Books, 2012], 91). She regards her calling more important than what the critics in the cheap seats have to say.

New Adapter Rachel Billups has taught me a lot about courageous leadership. When I met Rachel several years ago, she had recently been appointed as the senior pastor of a large historic church in Cincinnati. Rachel was twenty-nine years old. She was crossing boundaries that this church (and many for that matter) had never seen in their pastoral leadership. Namely, she was young and a woman. She was, though, committed to a God-given vision to lead this church from a season of decline to a place of new vitality, which included adding another site for worship. This work is not for the faint of heart. Rachel is not faint of heart. She is bold and caring. She is brave and sensitive to the leading of the Spirit. What happened at Shiloh United Methodist Church was, in my opinion, nothing short of a miracle. In a short time, the church experienced turn around, added another site, and embraced a young female pastor as their key leader. She faced critique but kept going. She listened to her detractors' comments and sought to understand them but at the same time did not let them keep her from leading the church forward. When I saw what God was able to do through her ministry, I realized the importance of moving forward even when the Back to Egypt Committee suggests you take a different path.

In the months before my wife, Rachel, and I launched Providence Church, we traveled as much as we could to learn from and hear from other leaders who had started successful ventures. We sought to talk to leaders who were twenty, thirty, forty years ahead of us. We noticed something. Many pastors and leaders over the years had grown hardened. After many battles in the arena, they had developed a really thick skin and a pretty sharp tongue. It was their way or the highway. They led well, but you could tell the wounds from the critics had made them tough. Some of them were just jerks.

On the other side we met some guys who were just punching the clock. Their wounds had made them numb. They had given up leading and adapting years ago and were on cruise control. They had become doormats and if you heard their stories, you wouldn't blame them.

Rachel and I openly talked about this dichotomy. It seemed there were two poles of leadership. We wondered which way we would tend and if there might be another way.

One day recently, I was fuming about some critics. Rachel and I stood in the kitchen, and I let her hear my prepared speeches to the ones who were breaking me down with their arrows of harsh critique. There was no question of which way I was headed that day. I was on the fast track to jerk-hood. (Other days, though, I would say I feel more like the quivering mass.) In the kitchen that day, Rachel grabbed my hand and made me look at her. (She's beautiful, remember.) She said, "Jacob Armstrong, I am praying for you a third way." I knew of the first and second way. We had talked of them often. "What is the third way?" I asked, still annoyed and focused on my critics. She said, "I am praying that you will abide in Christ. And in abiding you will be able to lead our church neither as doormat or jerk, but as strong and courageous, gentle and humble." I am convinced God speaks through others. That day God spoke through her.

It is one of the reasons I was drawn to Adam and Mike. Decades into the fight with countless letters of criticism that I know must have stung, they have sought a third way of leadership. One that is passionately devoted to Jesus. One that seeks to go his way. One that fails but picks itself back up. Time and time again.

I pray the third way for you as well. That you will listen more to the voice of God than to the voice of the Back to Egypt Committee. That you will keep going up the stairs into the arena, that you will keep walking toward the promised land.

A Conversation with Adam and Mike

Adam: This is a regular part of ministry. If you are going to be a leader, there will be people who don't like the way you lead. They won't like your haircut or something you said in a sermon, a position you take. You will be disappointing for people in some way.

During the debate leading up to the affordable care act, I said in a sermon that I believe this matters. That there are people who do not have health care and that it matters. We try not to use the pulpit as a political tool; we never say you have to vote this way or that way. But there were people who were very upset about that.

And one Sunday at the end of the services, I said to the congregation, "I give you room to disagree with me on this. That is always true, but I need to tell you that I have a picture in my mind that someday I will stand before Jesus, and he is going to say, 'I put you in a really big church and gave you a lot of influence, and you never said anything that was really important.' I fear disappointing Jesus more than I fear disappointing you." Every once in a while I think about that, and I screw up just enough courage to say something that I think needs to be said in that moment in time.

You have to examine what you're saying and how you're saying it. Because it is easier to irritate people than to influence people. And as pastors we need to be influencing. If we are just irritating, then something in us needs correction. If you want to influence people you must learn to speak their language. Some may still leave the church, but more will say, "I may not agree with you, but I appreciate the way you got me thinking about that."

Mike: And the gospel is offensive, and we can't shy away from that. It still hurts to lose people, though.

What also hurts is that you want people to get the whole gospel, and sometimes they've been with you a long time. Recently in a sermon on stewardship, I spoke about ethical treatment of workers and Isaiah 58. And I knew there would be people who will not want to be a part of that discussion. But I said at end of the message, I don't want you to stand before God and say your pastor didn't tell you! I think you know that more at sixty-three, when you are getting closer to the end of the journey, when you want to make sure you get it all in. I want to tell them the whole thing!

Adam: I remember the words of John 6:66. The scripture says, "At this, many of his disciples turned away." So you think, Jesus the Son of God was preaching and there were many who turned away.

Mike: And it says many of his disciples withdrew and turned away because they said this is too hard. This is too hard.

Adam: And sometimes they just leave because you were stupid. You preached a bad sermon and said what you shouldn't have said. And that will happen too. There have been times when I looked back and realized that if I had said that a little bit differently, those fifty people who left might be on the journey here still. They might have heard it and understood if I had been more careful and thoughtful in what I said and the way I said it. Sometimes we have bad judgment.

Chapter Six

GOOD-BYE TO THE SOLO, HEROIC LEADER

Moses had reached the end of his rope. He was crumbling emotionally under the weight of criticism and conflict. He was desperately weary from the years of going God knows where. There was too much on his plate and too much for him to handle. Anyone who has tried to lead people understands Moses's questions to God: "Did I conceive all these people? Did I give birth to them?" (Num 11:12). We relate to his emotional distress. "I can't bear this people on my own. They're too heavy for me" (Num 11:14). Then he asked God to kill him. He wanted God to kill him before the people killed him first. God had a different plan.

Remember that one of the lies of the Back to Egypt Committee is that *you have to do it on your own*. They put everything on Moses—all the responsibility and all the blame. God's plan, though, was to spread this out a bit.

In Numbers 11:16-17, "the LORD said to Moses, 'Gather before me seventy men from Israel's elders, whom you know as elders and officers of the people....I'll take some of the spirit that is on you and place it on them. Then they will carry the burden of the people with you so that you won't bear it alone.'"

God said Moses didn't have to do it all alone. God shared the burden of responsibility among many leaders. God established the idea of team ministry and team leadership in the wilderness. The example of Moses is that we need each other to effectively lead and live into God's vision for our community. But, unfortunately, the example of Moses wore off a long time ago.

For quite some time, the American church has lifted up a different ideal for leadership.

65

We returned to the solo, heroic leader.

He works eighty hours a week and never takes a day off. She sits at the hospital all day, attends every meeting each night, and writes her sermon sometime after midnight.

It sounds good and American, and most churches are just fine with it. But the solo, heroic leader is not a sustainable way of doing ministry, and it is an impossible ideal if you are interested in doing adaptive work. A high-capacity person can pull off a lot in this model, but they can't do the hard adaptive work that is necessary to take the church to a new place. There isn't enough time or energy left for it. If all a church wants a pastor to do is preach, teach, and visit, then a solo leader can pull that off. And if all a church wants their pastor to do is preach, teach, and visit, then the church is heading toward death.

I recently saw a pastor on Twitter say he had preached his 852nd consecutive Sunday. That is over sixteen years of preaching. My first thought was, *Wow, that's incredible.* My second thought was, *Boy, he must be tired.*

And that is the end result of the busy solo leader. They are really dang tired. Like, so tired it hurts. Normal criticism and conflict hurt worse because the tank is empty and the defenses are gone. So it follows that the leader is quickly wounded and oozing pessimism. The solo, heroic leader equals busy, tired, wounded leader.

In addition, solo, heroic leaders point all the attention on themselves. They are noticed and lauded and they breed other solo, heroic leaders to come up behind and around them who mimic their attention-seeking mentor. It gets ugly real quick.

The answer to the solo, heroic problems of fatigue, wounds, and arrogance is not just adding more people. That's what we tried when churches started to grow. We grew to a program-size church that had program staff to share the load. Having a church staff does not guarantee a change in the solo leader model. Most church staffs still operate in a very unintegrated manner. They gather for a two-hour staff meeting once a week, but it is only a quick huddle of solo leaders who have prayer together, review the calendar, and then go back out to work alone. These staff members or committees act as silos. They rarely integrate and work together.

My tone may sound critical at this point, but it is only because I have lived it and know how destructive this model can be. A few years into starting Providence Church I noticed my key lay leaders and staff—the ones who had begun full of energy, passion, and focus—were now increasingly busy, tired, and wounded. People started to burn out and there was more tension and conflict among us. In a meeting with one of our young, dynamic, hard-working staff members, I gave her a warning about burnout. I encouraged her to take care of herself, to share the burden with others, and to rest. I said that I wanted that for all of our leaders. What she said next I will never forget. She replied, "We will do that when you show us how."

John Donne, an Anglican priest and poet in the early seventeenth century, wrote, "*No man is an island, entire of itself; every man is a piece of the continent, a part of the main.*"

The paragraph ends with a famous line, "*and therefore never send to know for whom the bell tolls; it tolls for thee*" ("Meditation XVII" in Devotions upon Emergent Occasions [1959; Project Gutenberg, 2011], http://www.gutenberg.org/files/23772/23772-h/23772-h.htm).

I am not sure if Donne was thinking about leading and serving the church when he wrote his famous meditation, but when I was called upon to exemplify healthy leadership, not just coach it, I heard the bell tolling for me. It stunned me. I thought I had been modeling hard work (and I still value hard work and work hard), but I realize now I was modeling a form of arrogance that excluded other people from being a part of the amazing work of God. The chief cause of the burnout in our leaders was the example I had set. The bell tolled, and I heard it. I was not an island, but a part of the main, and that meant I had to change the way I worked and led. I had to adapt. My family, my ministry, and my life depended on it.

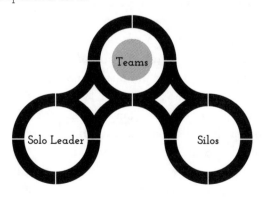

Teams

Teams save leaders from burnout. It is easy for a church to fall in love with a rock star leader. We all want a hero. But, in the words of my friend Wes Olds at Grace Church, "There is only one hero." (He's talking about Jesus.) When we act as a solo leader we set up a co-dependent relationship where the people want someone on a pedestal and the leader wants to be on a pedestal. The end result of this relationship is that the leader goes up in flames and the followers leave disappointed. Wes shared with me that he, like many of us, had been taught a model of leadership that exalted the one who could do it all and, while drawing the adulation of others, was left exhausted and empty. Wes wondered if there was another way and found it in the model of team leadership that now exists at Grace Church in Cape Coral, Florida. This amazing church was once declining and on its way to hospice care, before Jorge Acevedo came to be its pastor. Jorge, too, had been schooled in the solo, heroic model, and he went to work. After some years, though, Jorge began to implement a model of ministry that shared the burden and allowed teams to shoulder the weight of ministry. In a short time Grace has grown to four sites on three campuses. Their pastors serve long tenures and offer a model of sustainability to all who are in church leadership. The key is that they lead in teams. They trust each other, and they exhibit mutual submission. This leads to an environment where diverse voices are heard and valued, decisions are made quickly based on their ability to fulfill their mission, and they stay focused on reaching people for Christ. *And*, their leaders are healthy and looking forward to more years of ministry.

Teams make adaptive work possible. The types of adaptations mentioned previously in this book are almost impossible when attempted alone. Moving from old patterns of behavior to new ones requires collective reflection that a team provides. Moses could not get the people of God from Egypt to the promised land by himself. Imagine the changes in thinking and behavior needed to take a people from slavery to a new nation of freed people. As long as Moses acted as a solo leader, he would spend his time listening to grumbling, and all the while his frustration would build and the vision would leak.

One of the most adaptive, creative churches that I know is Urban Village Church. Currently with four locations in Chicago, they are on the leading edge of how multisite church can be done in an urban setting. What is most interesting to me, though, is how the church was started by not one but two pastors. Christian Coon and Trey Hall both carry the title of lead pastor, and they lead the church collaboratively with a team of people. It is significant that the church was started with a team leadership model, and I believe this is a key reason the church has been able to remain healthy, growing, and particularly adaptive in a very unique setting.

So, we build vision-centric teams whose purpose is not to carry out day-to-day work. Daily tasks are important and a part of any leader's job description. But, there must be times when the leaders gather in teams to see the bigger picture of where the church is headed. There must be a time when all the work can be viewed through the lens of the vision and difficult decisions can be made. At Providence, we have a clear vision that is read and discussed before any meeting of leaders. It drives what we do in the day to day because we take time as teams to reflect on what we are doing and make adjustments based on our vision.

These teams love, learn, and lead together. There are many different models for effective team leadership. Providence learned our model from an amazing group of Jesus followers in Lexington, Kentucky, called Spiritual Leadership, Inc. They are proponents of what they call an L3 model of team leadership. Teams love, learn, and lead together. We have found this to be the best way to abide in Christ, stay focused on the vision, and make the necessary changes along the journey.

> **Loving.** As spiritual leaders, we often forget that our own personal devotion to Christ is the most important thing we can do to lead others. If we aren't abiding in Christ, our people won't either. One of my mentors often tells me the church will only go as deep as you are. John Wesley wrote to his father in 1734, "My one aim in life is to secure personal holiness, for without being holy myself I cannot promote real holiness in others" (Howard Snyder, *The Radical Wesley and Patterns for Church Renewal* [Eugene, OR: Wipf & Stock, 1996], 14). Wesley, who took much time in personal devotion, also knew that it was in community that we best grow

in our commitment to Christ. All of his early leaders met in small groups for spiritual growth. Leadership teams in churches should devote time to loving God and loving each other. It sounds obvious but it is often neglected.

Learning. Leaders are learners. Teams that really want to see adaptive change happen are intent on learning together. They read together, discuss ideas, and pray about how it fits with their context. A pastor who reads the latest leadership books alone usually grows frustrated when no one else buys into his ideas. A team that learns together gleans from the wisdom that is out there and uses it to help their congregation grow.

Leading. When an adaptive team meets, they spend time loving God together, learning from each other, and facing the challenges that will allow them to continue to lead effectively. So often, our time is consumed with day-to-day tasks that keep us from doing what we were really called to do. When a team is formed to truly lead you will find that other leaders who were growing bored or burning out in day-to-day work are energized to do what they are actually gifted to do. Good leaders are also humble enough to know that they need help. Like Jorge and Wes at Grace Church, we employ a coach at Providence who helps us not get so mired in the day to day that we neglect to make sure we are heading in the right direction. Like a coach in athletics, someone who is not in the field of play can offer perspective and guidance that we can't see on our own.

Teams hold each other accountable. Teams also hold the venue for accountability. Here, I am not talking about the kind of accountability we usually think of in the church. The group that holds each other accountable for personal spiritual growth is one of importance and can be a part of the loving God time of an adaptive team. The accountability that is sorely lacking in the church today is about more, though, than helping each other stay focused on daily scripture reading or an exercise routine. Rarely do we hold each other accountable for staying focused on the vision (if we even have one) and simply for doing what we said we would do. Church leaders often spend exorbitant amounts of time setting out to do things that never get done. A team that loves, learns, and leads together provides a place for simple and faithful accountability around tasks that are critical for moving the church forward. Wes, who is the campus pastor at the Cape Campus of Grace Church, uses what he calls a playbook with his team. In the playbook are clearly outlined objectives for the future, metrics to measure them, and owners of each goal. This allows the team to hold each other accountable to that which they agreed was important for the mission.

Teams create other teams. We often marvel at the exponential growth of the early church. Twelve followers of Jesus took the good news to the world. A more recent example is the growth of the church in China. For almost a century the church was illegal and yet grew like wildfire behind closed doors. How? Small groups of people gathered who then started more small groups. I believe the future of our churches growing will be in small groups of people who then start other small groups. This will start with the leadership. Teams must be generative.

A little over a year ago, we noticed a gap in our church. It was heard in the murmuring of our people, but it was really uncovered in a leadership team who loves, learns, and leads together. Our new church that had grown rapidly was struggling to care for each other. At the time, we had two pastors who were seeking to provide congregational care for hundreds in a model that was not sustainable. Without the leadership team we would have continued to do the day-to-day tasks of calls, visits, and follow-ups and continued to know we were doing an inadequate job with no hope of doing anything different. Our leadership team, though, regularly talked about this gap and prayed about how to adaptively change. A team of laypeople was established: the Providence care team. They met for many months, loving God together, learning from others, and discerning a vision for caring for our new congregation and our community. A year later the care team has grown into many teams that are caring for people. There is a team that provides meals to those who need food in times of crisis, a team that cares for growing families that have grown either through birth or adoption, a team that provides items for waiting rooms at hospitals, a team that knits and prays over shawls that are delivered to the sick and wounded, a team that cares for the grieving, a team that visits the homebound and hospitalized, even a team that provides transportation to those who can no longer drive. And more! Before as pastor and solo leader, I had provided a bottleneck that prevented care from happening. I was tired, and the congregation was suffering. When I stepped out of the way and empowered other leaders who held gifts for care, the Providence care team grew from one team into many.

Clearly a common denominator in the great movements of God's people has been a team of people focused on the vision God has given them. We see it with Moses sharing the burden. We see it in Jesus gathering a team to carry out his public ministry. We see it in Paul's letters as he begins his letters by naming those on his team who travel with him. We see it in John Wesley, who traveled with a team of people who birthed the Methodist movement. We usually only put one person's statue up on a pedestal, but rarely can the success of a movement be traced to a solo leader.

We have already looked at one biblical image for the church, the bride of Christ, to which we will return later. The other central image is one of a body. Indeed it seems Donne was thinking of the church when he wrote his famous meditation about our need for connection. No doubt, he knew well the words, "You are the body of Christ and parts of each other" (1 Cor 12:27). In the same way as a body part isolated from the rest of the body is useless, so we lose our power and effectiveness when we disconnect from the main.

I have no doubt God has called you to something big, but you will not do it alone. That you must do it alone is an old lie that you will hear. Don't believe it.

A Conversation with Adam and Mike

Adam: Ministry and leadership change over time, along with the size and other characteristics of your church. At the very beginning, one other person and I were doing everything. Sharpening pencils, putting out attendance notebooks, delivering coffee mugs, making every hospital call, and all the rest. Pretty soon it got to a point where I could not get things done that were really critical. I realized I had to get help. And so I began asking people, and I found that people wanted to help, to be needed, and they wanted to be involved in ministry. I thought I had to do it all! And every time I'd give away something—like when I stopped delivering coffee mugs to every first time visitor and instead tapped volunteers to do this—it about killed me. I felt like "this is my job" and I love doing it. But other people could do the work just as well as I could. And another example is hospital calls. We have teams of people who are trained, who go out and make hospital calls. As another example, I used to do every wedding and every funeral, and now we have other pastors who are doing that. I remember the first time I did not do a wedding for a member. It was hard. And even worse the first time I didn't do a funeral for a member.

You surround yourself with great staff, when you can free up the resources, to support the ministries and the laypeople. But before we had staff, laypeople were doing it all. Today we find that the staff is making possible the ministry of the laity. The staff is training and equipping people to successfully do ministry. We unleash the power of the church when we send out laypeople to use their gifts, to be engaged in ministry.

And in pastoral care alone, we would need more than 250 clergy to take care of our congregation if only pastors were giving care. Instead, we have all these great laypeople who go through intensive training to do this ministry, and they are energized and excited and they do a great job—a better job sometimes than overly busy pastors ever could.

Mike: We call ours care networkers, and last year they made over ten thousand contacts. Now how many staff would it take to do that? We could never afford it, by any means.

Adam: You have to ask, "Where can I have the most impact?" There are certain things that you have to do, that only you can do. It might be somewhat different from pastor to pastor, although much of it is the same. Vision casting, preaching, reaching out into the community on behalf of the church, raising money—those are things that Mike and I both have to do, that we all have to do as pastors. But there are other things that I do really well, and still other things that Mike does really well, and he's going to be the best person to do that in his church, and likewise for me. It's true for every pastor. We've each got to decide where our time and effort is likely to have the most significant impact.

Chapter Seven

NO MORE TURF

When I arrived in Mt. Juliet, Tennessee, to start a new church, not everyone was happy about it. I had heard at the church planting trainings I had attended that it was common for existing churches to feel some uneasiness in a new church being started in their area. My coach told me to expect it. For some reason, though, I figured my experience would be different. I grew up in Mt. Juliet. I was the hometown boy. Jesus said something about how we should expect to be received in our hometown, but I wasn't thinking about that.

My first Sunday, I was invited to preach at Grace United Methodist Church, the largest UMC in Mt. Juliet and my home church. Dr. Ron Brown, the senior pastor then, had been gracious and encouraging to me in the weeks leading up to my move. As we were putting our robes on before the first of three services Ron said, "Jacob, not everybody is happy about this."

"They're not?" I asked.

"No," he said. "Some people are quite upset." We prayed and processed into worship.

My anxiety was rising as the service went on. I had been told a church planter needed thick skin, and I knew mine was paper-thin. And this wasn't just some church; this was my church, the people who had raised me and taught me. I would have no faith without them. "Some people are quite upset." The phrase pulsed in my brain as I tried to remember my sermon.

And then, before I was to preach, Ron stood up and walked to the center of the stage. Ron is a gentle but powerful leader, and he did not mince words. "Church," he said, "we are starting a new church." A hush fell over the crowd. "We get to be a part of it. It's not about us and them. It's about the kingdom. If you feel called to go, you have our blessing to go. If you feel called to give your money, God will provide what we need. We will support this young man and his team in any way we can."

I heard people before, when referring to how churches should be in relationship, say, "We are all on the same team." I had heard that before, but I had never seen it until Ron showed me. In fact, most all of my experience before and after has shown me that the church does not operate as if we are on the same team. Not at all. We have duplicate ministries, have little to no communication, and act as if we are on separate islands in the same community.

That day and in the weeks that followed I saw how the courage of one leader could connect churches together in a way that leads to powerful results.

Nine months later, on the Sunday before Providence Church officially launched, Grace UMC held a baby shower. Replete with streamers and a cake, it was quite a party. A baby was being born, a new church. The proud mother, Grace, gave us quite a sending off.

A key adaptation for the church moving forward is moving from competition and comparison to collaboration and respect. No more turf, and that means no more turf wars. Once we eschew the enemies of competition and comparison, the floodgates for beautiful partnerships are opened and the people of God together can see the transforming power of Christ unleashed on a community. So beware of these killers…competition and comparison. They are regular companions in the business world and the sporting arena. They lurk in the middle school hallways and are constant in marketing.

Competition is not always a bad thing and being aware of what others are up to is a good idea. But we must acknowledge that for some of us in the church, competition and comparison are not helpful at all. They lead to anxiety, frustration, and, at times, paralysis.

Numbers used to cause me great anxiety and became a great source of distraction. When I realized that most of my fixation on numbers was not about furthering God's vision for me and the church but about how I compared with others, I began to ask God to free me from that. When we remember that each context is different and every faithful expression of ministry is of value to God, we can feel the hold that competition and comparison has on us begin to loosen.

New Adapters, focused on the vision God has given, are not competitive or paralyzed by comparison. Instead they look for ways to collaborate with other believers that will lead to a furtherance of the vision. At the same time, they are respectful of how others think about and do ministry differently. Respect begins in our hearts, but it moves quickly to our mouths. We must speak respectfully about other churches and pastors and pass a culture of cooperation down to those who serve with us.

Here are some ways that New Adapters can collaborate and respect ministry partners in their area.

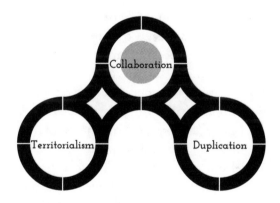

Collaboration

Churches start new churches. For a long time the task of starting churches has fallen to the large ones. They are seen as having the financial resources and human power to make it happen. They have the bandwidth for such a large undertaking. I think that it is not the size of a church that is critical for planting, but the health of the church that should be considered. Every healthy church, regardless of size, should be thinking about how they can help create new Jesus communities.

Providence was started not by one church, but by a group of large and small churches that believed a United Methodist church was needed in a new community. In the months before Providence launched

I visited each church. A large county seat church gave a significant financial gift while also supplying worship attenders to our preview services. Another large suburban church gave emotional and financial support to Rachel and me. Smaller churches that I visited with felt just as involved in our planting. They were our key prayer supporters, banding together to pray and receiving regular notifications of special prayer requests for the new church. As I mentioned, Grace, the closest UMC, stepped up in a big way by sending pioneers to join us and by providing a home base for us in our first year. It is common for us to hear of five or six churches who consider themselves one of the "mother" churches of Providence. We love that! Even though our church has grown significantly, these churches still help us on a regular basis by providing our mobile congregation with space for meeting, classes, and services.

Four years into the life of Providence Church, our pastor of connections, Holley Potts, began to feel a call to plant in her city. She and her husband lived in a neighboring community. We had a number of church members who made the drive and small groups that met already in her town. At first, we wondered how a four-year-old church could start a new church on its own. We decided "on our own" was indeed not the best way! Holley and another pastor began to form partnerships with other churches and people in that community as well as soliciting support from our conference. Now a vibrant new church exists in a nearby community with one of our former pastors and quite a few of our folks. We don't claim credit for it; we really can't! But we played a key role by providing what we could to help this new Jesus community begin. On the Sunday before they launched, we held a send-off for them!

I believe all healthy churches should consider how they can be a part of planting new Jesus communities. We all have something that we can offer to an effort that will lead new people to Christ.

Churches should engage in mission together. For too long, churches have done community outreach in isolation. Duplicate ministries exist in churches that if consolidated could serve the people of an area more effectively. But, since we disagree on baptism or because it feels good to get all the credit, we remain separate. This isn't faithful, and we need to stop. We need courageous leaders who will be willing to adapt the old model of isolated ministry to a new one of collaboration and respect. There should be no illusion that we will all agree on everything. I fit comfortably in a Wesleyan theology; others don't. I don't agree with what all the folks mentioned in this book say or believe. But, I love them and know that together we are much stronger and a more powerful force for the mission I know we all do agree on: making disciples of Jesus Christ for the transformation of the world. Likewise, we should look beyond some of the differences we have with sisters and brothers in our community so that we can achieve more together than we can apart.

An audit of other churches and their ministries will allow you to learn two things. One, you will see areas of duplication where you can bind together to be a more powerful force. Two, you will see things being done beautifully well that you can feel confident in not doing so that you can do something else that fits the gifts of your church. There is a wonderful, missional church in our community that started around the same time as Providence. Friendship Community Church and their pastor Todd Stevens are doing amazing work for Christ, and Todd and I have become friends. Over the last two years, Todd and his wife, Erin, have established an amazing and life-transforming ministry that they call Strip Church. They care for and minister to the dancers in the local strip clubs. When I first heard about this, I was blown away by such an incredible way of being the church. It seemed like something Jesus would do. I wondered how we could be involved or do something like that ourselves. Then I realized that they've got this for now. What is God calling us to do? Instead of replicating the ministry of our sister churches, let's replicate the process of prayer and discernment that led them to such a unique calling. It was about the same time Todd and Friendship were beginning their unique ministry that we felt God leading us to be a church that is intentional about caring for families of children of special needs in our community, and off we went. We should engage in mission together when that makes sense and engage in mission in the community in the way that we are called without having to replicate everyone else's ministry.

Churches should partner together in ways that promote our strengths and acknowledge our weaknesses. Providence Church has a lot to offer our community. We don't, though, have a building. We do not have a facility and all the things that a facility offers a community. It is a current weakness. We focus on our strengths. We partner with churches in ways that help promote both entities' strengths as we acknowledge our weaknesses. A nearby church, Dodson Chapel, is situated in a community that is filled with children. This church of forty members bought an abandoned public school and runs a childcare for the community out of it. We were drawn to this amazing ministry and dreamed together how we could partner together. We have a bunch of people who care about children; they have the location and facility to do that work. We have over the years been a group that does repairs on the building, helps keep their playgrounds up to code, and hosts outreach ministries on their campus. Last summer, Providence Church (a church with no building) held its Vacation Bible School on the grounds of Dodson Chapel, an urban church surrounded by hundreds of unreached families. It was a benefit to both churches as we promoted our strengths and acknowledged our weaknesses. At Providence Church we do graphic art and printed materials really well. That is why for two years we have done the bulletins for Dodson Chapel. During that time, they have let our youth group use their buses. It just makes sense! We are all on the same team.

Resurrection Downtown, pastored by Scott Chrostek, began their church in an older urban congregation's sanctuary. For their first year, they worshiped on Sunday nights in a room used by another church on Sunday mornings. It just makes sense! We are all on the same team. Competition and comparison kills these types of partnerships before they even start, but a heart toward collaboration and respect leads to all types of possibilities.

More in-depth partnerships are possible when both churches believe in the mission to reach new people. Over the last decade especially, New Adapters have seen the amazing possibilities when healthy churches partner with struggling or dying churches. It takes great intentionality and prayer but when carefully handled can lead to amazing results. Mike and Adam have been leaders in these types of partnerships as we have already heard. One thing that can be gleaned is that there is no "one way" to partner with or restart a congregation. There are, though, some common factors:

There must be clear leadership and vision coming from the healthy organism. The leaders of the sending church must be in one voice regarding belief in and support of the new entity. If a new church is trying to be started in an existing church and leadership from the sending church is not of one accord, there will be many pitfalls along the way. It would be better to focus clearing up where everyone stands or starting the new church a different way.

There must be a season of discernment and prayer on the part of both churches that leads to a common hope to see new life happen and new people reached. The same type of process described in chapter 1 must happen in the new community. The healthy church cannot just come and do exactly what they do at their main campus. They must be careful in learning from the new community and establish a new ministry that encompasses the assets of that community.

The older congregation must be willing to change, in some ways die, and be reborn. Wes Olds at Grace Church in Cape Coral, Florida, who has been a part of several successful restarts, says, "There must be a willingness to lay down practices that put the church in a state of decline." It is for this reason that Grace has had several other conversations with dying congregations that have not led to a partnership. Wes says that "everything must be on the table" and then new life comes. This may be the most difficult part of partnering, but it is essential.

Competition and comparison keep these things from happening. (Have I mentioned that yet?) If you are competitive like me, then you need to get that out in Monopoly games with your kids or during church softball games. Don't take it out on the precious faithful in your community who share the same hope as you. No more turf.

Remember that one of Jesus's last hopes for us is that we "will be one" (John 17:23). We hear that often, but we rarely remind each other why Jesus had that hope for us. He compared his hope for our unity with each other to the way that he and his Father related, and he said he prayed for unity in the hopes that "the world will know that you sent me." Man, I hope I don't let my sinful desire to be the best or win the race keep the world from believing that God sent Jesus.

A Conversation with Mike and Adam

Mike: We have a Pentecostal church near us, and the pastor there is a great guy. Our theology may be somewhat different, but we are one in Jesus. He asked us to partner with them to fight heroin use. We have a terrible heroin problem in Dayton. We partnered with this church, and the pastor e-mailed and suggested that our churches do more together. That excites me, and it's something I think is important that we have not paid much attention to.

On the other hand, when you consider reviving or restarting an existing church, you must remember that you can't breed health in the midst of ill health. We've found that the unhealthy church has to agree to basically shut down, to agree to have no more mechanism for voting on changes or actions as a church. If they are able to agree to that, only then can we place people for leadership and do what we know needs to be done to restart the church in a healthy state.

This Pentecostal church has really become one of our competitors, in a sense. It is large and sophisticated. I am thankful that people are finding Jesus in a variety of ways and places. Some people have left our church to go to that one, and we have to see that as an exciting thing. We have to humble ourselves and see these partnerships as a positive step for the kingdom.

Adam: All of us are a little insecure. It doesn't matter who you are or how successful you've been, there is a little insecurity in each of us. I think we all secretly fear that someone is going to figure out that we're really not that great. As you grow in Christ, that insecurity becomes smaller and smaller. But when you first start off on ministry it is so easy to see others as competitors. Every one of you is trying to reach those young people, those older people, those families, *all* people.

And as Christians we should celebrate every time that that happens, wherever it happens.

We found as a congregation that if we intentionally aimed to bless other churches, it was good for them and for us. From the time we started Resurrection with ninety people, we cast a vision that anything we learned we would give it away. That became part of our DNA. We are about renewing churches. And when we were small, people snickered at that, like "What do you think you can teach us? You're a twenty-five-year-old kid with ninety people, and you think you're going to teach us anything?" But I felt like God could somehow use us to renew the denomination, and I tried to wire that into our congregation. We were proud to be United Methodists, and I wanted our people not to be boastful but to see themselves as part of something that could renew the Methodist movement. As we did learn things and give things away, we did it with humility. We don't have all the answers. And we want to know what is happening at other churches, all the amazing ministries happening elsewhere, too. But if there is something we can give away that will help another church, we want to do it.

You realize you are blessed to be a blessing. As you are able, your ministry should increasingly be about what you can give away, how you can encourage congregations, equip other leaders. God blesses that, I think. To whom much is given, Jesus said, much is expected. I found years ago it was common to dis the denomination. People were dissing the bishops and the boards and agencies, the seminaries. This still happens a lot. People speak negatively about the movement now just as they did twenty-five years ago. We decided to speak positively about it, to be a cheerleader. People accused me of being a Pollyanna and asked if I really believed that the denomination's best years could be ahead of it. And I told people then and tell people now that I'm going to believe and speak about it until it happens.

I'm not Pollyanna. I just think that if we speak positively, and give good things away, if we are gracious and kind, and if we speak well even of people with whom we disagree, God joins us in that and blesses it.

Mike: The Fort McKinley neighborhood transitioned in the 1960s. It had been filled with housing built in the 1940s for General Motors employees. Then the jobs left, and the neighborhood transitioned. There were about forty elderly white people left in the church, who'd moved away in the '60s but kept coming to the church. There wasn't a child left in the building. The Sunday school rooms had become storage rooms. But they had one thing going for them: a distant memory of mission. In the 1980s a friend of mine was pastor there and began to renew the congregation's sense of mission. Then she was appointed as a district superintendent. But she left the people with that glimmer of an idea about mission. We went in and sent laypeople at first, so that this little congregation could see what it looks like for laypeople to be leaders and to be in mission. Soon there were people showing up. And then there were five, seven, then ten kids showing up. The congregation took a vote and became part of Ginghamsburg. We changed the worship and music styles to reach the unchurched people in the neighborhood. We also started tutoring programs in the neighborhood schools. We could not have achieved this if that handful of people had not retained their memory of mission. The concept of mission has to be present—even if it's been dormant for years—in order for this sort of missional transformation to happen. It is important to understand this when you're considering the restart of an existing congregation.

Chapter Eight

RAISING UP NEW AND YOUNG LEADERS

Rosario Picardo started Embrace Church in an old theater in Lexington, Kentucky, in 2009. In 2014, he left Embrace to become the executive pastor of new church development at Ginghamsburg Church. What happened between 2009 and 2014 is worth careful examination. Roz didn't leave Embrace because he was seeking a better opportunity. He didn't leave because the church plant had been a failure and it was time to throw in the towel and move on. He left because Embrace was good without him. Roz had done the hard work of creating a culture that wasn't centered on him. He cultivated leaders from the people he came to reach. From day one, he was intent on raising up new and young leaders to carry the church when he moved on. Five years in, the church of four distinct worshipping communities was left in more than capable hands. John Gallaher, the new lead pastor of Embrace, was not someone shipped in from another place. John was a current leader on the Embrace team. He had preached once a month for the last three years. For five years Rosario had been looking for the Faithful, Available, and Teachable. FAT leaders, he calls them, are the ones you want. Give them exposure and give them face time. See if they will serve and watch them grow.

New Adapters are raising up new and young leaders. The old model of ministry of paying your dues and hoping to get a chance for a key leadership position when you are more seasoned is over. This doesn't mean that seasons of growth and intentional mentoring are over; it just means that new leaders must be given a chance to actually lead earlier. If not, we will miss them and lose them. With long and tedious ordination processes and a lack of clarity in how young people gain opportunity in most of our denominations, the church has for a while been missing on gifted and called leaders. New Adapters are remedying this by allowing new and young leaders to learn on the job, allowing them to fail, and then empowering them to carry on.

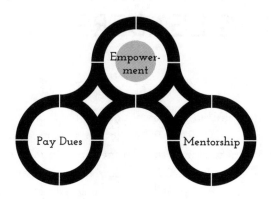

Empowerment

Don't be threatened by it. Rosario taught me that the first step in raising up new leaders and handing off leadership is getting over our insecurities and our need to get all the attention. Even if you are threatened by it a bit, give it a try. The more you do it, the more you will get used to it. At times, we are worried we will work ourselves out of a job by intentionally mentoring people who are more gifted and talented than us. Sometimes we are threatened by the youthful energy and enthusiasm that we see lacking in ourselves. The converse, though, is really true. If we don't intentionally mentor people who are more gifted than ourselves, we will create a system dependent on us that is destined to fail. Thus, the demise that I so fear becomes reality because of my inability to create a system that doesn't bottleneck with me. It is also true that the energy and enthusiasm of our juniors will give fire to flames that we forgot were burning in us.

In 2008, Mike and Adam began the Young Pastors Network, calling together young leaders from all across the country to learn from them. One of the first things they told us is that they believed their future replacements could be in the room. Instead of being threatened by that, they chose to pass down what they had learned even though they were still many years from their retirements. Both Adam and Mike are surrounded by supremely talented leaders. Instead of threatening, it invigorates them for the new challenges ahead. Young leaders are not resistant to mentoring and oversight. In contrast to their baby boomer parents, young leaders lack the ingrained distrust and disdain for those older than them. Instead, they crave mentoring and oversight. They don't want to wait to do the work, but they do want someone alongside them to guide and teach them.

We must make risky investments in new leaders. Our investments in new and young leaders can't be a small part of what we do. Our investments also cannot be safe. Investments are always risky. They don't always work out. But, we must invest in new leaders if we truly care about the mission. We must risk time, energy, and money. We risk losing attention and recognition that might have come our way. We risk losing some control. Right now we have a twenty-seven-year-old pastor on our staff, a recent seminary graduate, who feels a call to plant a new church. She is serving with us while on a one-year residency partially funded by our denominational arm for church planting. We are investing together in Erica believing she will be a part of changing the world for Christ. We only have twelve months together. That is why in her first month out of seminary she preached at Providence before over one thousand people. I was there. It was awesome. Her purpose in preaching wasn't spelling me so I could take vacation. Her purpose in preaching was bringing the gospel to people who desperately need it and need to hear it from different voices. I can't let my codependent need of being needed keep me from making the necessary investments in new leaders so my church and others can thrive long after I'm gone.

Know ahead of time that their way of leading will be different from yours. This is the hardest one. It hurts the worst. New leaders won't do things the way you did them. They might even do them better and other people might even like them better than you. A part of adapting is recognizing that the church will have to be led in different ways. A friend of mine from my childhood, Ingrid McIntyre, like me, went to seminary soon after college. Like me, she was captivated by a desire to live her life for Jesus in a way that made an impact. After seminary, though, she did not find a ready-made spot for her in the church to live out her call. So, instead of entering ordained ministry, she hit the streets. Literally. She served and lived among the displaced and homeless in Nashville, most notably after many homeless communities were washed away in the flood of 2010. Ingrid was relentless in her desire to bring basic needs to the people who needed them, and she was unapologetic about the church's need to do it. She established a non-profit, Open Table Nashville, that disrupts cycles of poverty, journeys with the marginalized, and provides education about issues of home-lessness. Open Table was recently featured on *60 Minutes*, with An-derson Cooper taking a trip with Ingrid to meet a man who lived in a storage facility. The feature followed the man from living in a garage to having his own apartment. Ingrid, a new leader for a new time, had no clear designation or place in the old institution of United Methodism. It is why I considered it a mark of great leadership and courage when Bishop Bill McAlilly licensed Ingrid as a United Methodist pastor and appointed her to the streets of Nashville. This had not been done before, but our times require us to do things we have never done before.

The new leaders you invest in will have vision for ways of do-ing ministry that don't fit our current models. It is in these times that we have to stretch or even break our models to allow new leaders to emerge.

After we invest, **we have to let them go**. I mentioned in the last chapter that we let our beloved Pastor Holley go. We didn't have much choice. She was going anyway. But we embraced her call to plant Mercy Street United Methodist Church in her community and sent her out with love and support. My inclination as pastor of Provi-dence would have been to keep this talented member of our team as long as we could. Denominational reports would not show that Provi-dence had grown after the new church was planted; in fact we had a decrease in both attendance and giving as members of our church went to help plant with Holley. Big deal. We got over it. Maybe we won't win an award this year. After investing in new leaders we have to let them go. Like Rosario at Embrace, sometimes those leaders become our replacements, other times they become key leaders at our church, and other times they go somewhere else.

Not all new leaders are young. Becky Yates came to our church in our first few weeks of worshipping. Becky had enjoyed a successful career in publishing and now in her early fifties came to a Providence service only to appease the constant invitations from a coworker. Becky did not want to help start a church; she had done that before. She didn't want to come to a more contemporary church; she loved singing in the choir. She didn't want to come, but she did. In her first service with us, we concluded with a song that said something to the effect of "I will do more than just sing." Becky felt God calling her to stay. What I didn't know then was that as an eleven-year-old girl, in a denomination that did not affirm women to serve in ministry roles, Becky had felt a call to serve and do mission work. Life took her another route, and after raising four young children as a single mom and having a career in a secular field, God led her to an elementary school gym and a church committed to service and mission. Becky is full of energy and tenacity, and I'm pretty sure could beat me in arm wrestling. Becky became our first staff person devoted to outreach and is now in the process of becoming a United Methodist pastor. We invested in her, but more so she invested in us. On a staff of all twenty- and thirtysomethings, Becky brings a perspective and wisdom that we sorely need. I have a feeling that soon we will let her go as she will be sent out to live more fully into her call as a pastor. Just a reminder that not all new leaders are young.

Leading in the church today isn't about paying your dues and climbing your way up the ladder. It is about investing, empowering, and letting go.

—o—O—o—

A Conversation with Adam and Mike

Adam: Whether we like it or not, vibrant, healthy churches typically require a leader that the people in that community can connect with. And they require passionate leaders who are in love with Jesus Christ and passionate about people, who love them and are effective in organizing them and leading them to do kingdom work in the world. If The United Methodist Church is to have a future, it will not be because of some program launched at any general board or agency, as important as those are, and I believe in our boards and agencies. The single most important thing that must happen if the UM is to have a future is gifted pastors inviting gifted young people to listen for God's voice and God's call in their lives.

We have around 950 clergy under the age of thirty-five in the denomination. We will see wave after wave of people retiring in the next ten to fifteen years, losing about 60 percent of our clergy. So there will come a point in time when we see a clergy shortage even with the churches that are consolidating. But it's not about the clergy shortage. It's about starting new missions and new works. At Resurrection, we recognize that our church is in part here because a bishop appointed a twenty-five-year-old guy to go start a church. It was God's work, but it required somebody who didn't know you couldn't do it. Somebody who was young enough to not know it couldn't be done. We've got to find people like that. When you're young, you are reaching people who are young. You're willing to try things that other people wouldn't think to do. I know you slow down when you're fifty and older. I'm slower now than I was when I was twenty-five. There are things I'm better at, wiser about, and smarter at, and there are other things that I don't do as well now as I did when I was twenty-five. We have to recognize this.

Mike: At Ginghamsburg we are working on a plan to start one thousand new churches by 2050. I'm sixty-three years old. I have to build a team that can live into this future. Currently on our staff we have three pastors age thirty-four, thirty-three, and thirty-one. I am investing in them to help us live into this future. I believe that leadership is a gift, that there are some who are anointed for it. I look to identify these leaders and then invest in them. When I was young, there were those who invested in me and empowered me to do what we have done. I am investing in young leaders at Ginghamsburg to help us move into a future that I won't be around for. My investment is not just in their professional lives. It is an investment in their spirits and characters.

ISN'T SHE LOVELY?

I stood alone at the altar of a dimly lit chapel in a rented tuxedo. I was waiting for my bride.

We were young. Not young like it's-weird-and-our-parents-have-to-sign-the-paperwork young, but young nonetheless. She was twenty. I, the elder, stood six days past my twenty-first birthday. Somehow in our barely adult minds and hearts everything had pointed to us making this grand commitment to each other. For the past three years it was as if we had thought and talked of nothing else. At first, in whispered conversations that were known only to us, and then as time passed we let others in on the great secret of our intended pledge.

Despite all that is impractical about getting married when you are twenty and twenty-one (let me count the ways...), Rachel and I were and remain pretty practical people. So practical, in fact, that we decided to forego the usual wonder and surprise that accompanies seeing your bride for the first time when she walks down the aisle during the wedding ceremony. We liked the idea of that moment, but practically it didn't make sense. If we waited for "the moment" we would not be able to take any pictures together until after the wedding, causing all of our invited guests to do the long wait at the reception until we arrived. Being practical, we decided we would forego the moment with the comfort and time of our guests in mind.

So, we decided to stage the moment. We agreed to meet early in a little side chapel of the historic church where hours later the real ceremony would take place.

She walked in the back door, and my life changed forever. Her beauty was overpowering and was made even a little more surreal by our fancy clothes and dim lighting. It felt like make-believe as we wore our costumes and held hands wordless. We were married a few hours later, but we promised each other in that little chapel with an electric organ and teal carpet that we were in this for the long haul.

We've only journeyed thirteen years from that day, but it has been enough time for both of us to change. There are few who don't change dramatically from twenty to thirty-three. (I have a few buddies who haven't, but that is a different story.) Rachel and I have experienced a ton of wonderful things together and a handful of devastating ones. We have seen some of our dreams come true and a few others crumble to the ground. She is even more dazzlingly beautiful now. My hair has completely turned gray. She still makes me laugh. I still ache when she is away. We are stronger than we were a decade ago, with a few more bumps and bruises than we probably would have imagined.

You can take any metaphor too far, and I feel I'm pushing the limits on this one (as mentioned before, the primary metaphor for the church in the New Testament is the body of Christ, and you can tease that one a bit more than this one), but if I can understand from my experience of having a gorgeous bride just a hint of what Jesus meant when he said we were his bride, I can say this: we should be very slow to think that just because the church is imperfect and wounded that we are anything less than beautiful to him.

The other night I met with a young family in my office. Chris wore a ball cap and the cool kind of beard that thirty-year-old guys wear these days. Stephanie had in her eyes that mixture of light and fatigue that only a new mom does. I could tell that Savannah, age eight, had something on her mind she wanted to share, while her brother David, only a few months old, sang a baby song of burps and coos.

I started with Savannah. "Why are you guys here tonight?"

Her rehearsed answer came out with ease. "Pastor Jacob, I want to be baptized."

"Fantastic," I said. "Why do you want to be baptized, Savannah?"

"I believe in God and Jesus," she replied. I knew it was going to be a good night. Savanah and I talked about baptism, and I believed her to be duly prepared. Then, Chris and Stephanie asked about infant baptism because they had seen it practiced in our church. I explained that it was an ancient ritual that acknowledged the work of God's grace in our lives long before we could ever even respond.

Chris shared with me that he had not grown up in church and in his twenties had been focused on anything but God. He said now he woke up on Sundays excited to come to church. He sensed God's presence there and a pull on his life for more.

Stephanie shared that she had been baptized as an infant in the Catholic Church but had little connection to the church since then. A friend, though, had invited her to a silent retreat hosted by our church. There, she said, she encountered God and prayed for the first time in a long time. That led them to give our church a try, and now here they were in my office because Savannah says she believes in God and Jesus.

I realized I was talking to a family just like mine had been three decades before. I was the young pastor who got to share about the grace of God and invite them to be a part of the church just like my first pastor had done in 1980.

I sent my team an e-mail that night after they left.

Hey guys,
   Just met with a family. Dad shared how he had never wanted to go to church and hadn't until Providence. Now he wakes up on Sundays excited to go. Mom shared how she didn't grow up in church, but after a time of emptiness went to a Silent Retreat and there encountered God! On Sunday, Mom and Dad will make profession of faith in Jesus, 8 year old daughter will be baptized, and 7 month old son will have his infant baptism as they promise to raise him in the church.
   Thanks for believing in our vision to see those who feel disconnected from God and the church find hope, healing, and wholeness in Jesus Christ.
   Jesus said he came to seek and save the lost. He is persistent and committed to that work. He never gives up. We won't either.
   Love you guys, Jacob

That Sunday, Savannah was baptized in an old cattle trough that we fill from the faucet in the janitor's closet next to our middle school gym. And before I sprinkled water on baby David's head and made the sign of the cross on his forehead...

I asked his parents if they repented of their sin and acknowledged the power God gives to release them from sin.

They professed their faith in Jesus as Savior and Lord.

And, interestingly, in the ancient liturgy of the church, they professed their belief in the church that God has opened to people of all ages, nations, and races.

We get to be a part of Christ's work. So close to him in it that, like a marriage, we are one flesh.

Christ's church. Jesus's bride. Us.

Isn't she lovely?

Final Thoughts from Adam and Mike

Mike: It's humbling for Adam and me to sit here, to hear these New Adapters name specific things that we've influenced in their lives. And you look back and say, well if I had just chosen a different path, maybe made a lot of money, I would have missed out on so much. I would have missed helping people in extraordinary ways. That's a big thing.

I'm sixty-three, and at Ginghamsburg we are focusing on how we can plant one thousand new faith communities by 2050. I told Adam recently, you've got to be called, because you work Saturdays, Sundays, holidays. The only way you can do this is to be called and to keep dreaming the future, what God is doing in the future. And also realize that you are just being faithful in your part of the future. God's got something ahead of you, too. You are running your leg of the race, and you want to do it right.

This is the best thing going. I'm the oldest person at this table, and I still say this is amazing. My wife and I pass that little country church building, the original Ginghamsburg Church, and I say, I don't know how this happened. I know the who and the why, but I don't know how.

Adam: Part of why we wanted to be part of this conversation is that we want to invest in all of you who are New Adapters. You're doing something important, and we want to know what we can do to help. We want to help all of you who are on this path or starting to approach it. I just feel energized sitting here listening to each of you talk about what is going on in your ministries and your lives. It is so cool.

Mike: You are the leaders, the future.

Adam: Each of you in your own setting—it is so fun to watch and to follow what all of you are doing. It is so interesting to see the ups and downs, the ways that you all are doing new things. It is especially good to see old churches that have closed and been restarted, with ministries that really connect with the communities they're in. It is so good to see the work that some of you are doing to give old congregations a future with hope. It is hard, harder to raise the dead than to give birth to something new. I'm so thankful for what you all are doing in all of these different places.

Mike: Let's be like Wesley, committed to the church but not building a movement that is dependent on the church. It is resistant to change and full of divisions. I'm committed to it, and I don't see how it lasts with its resistance to change. But God will do something new, just like God's always done.

I love The United Methodist Church based on its theology. It's one of the only places that would have me. I believe in the literal resurrection of Jesus. I believe in the apostolic faith. But at the same time I believe that Jesus said when the Spirit comes, he will lead you into things that will come. We are people of the Spirit. And through holy conferencing we discover new things about ourselves and God and how we relate to one another.

Adam: Listening to you New Adapters and other new and young pastors gives me great hope. Because I see that God is raising up new people. The young elders I'm meeting are gifted and passionate, and they give me hope. And the fact that many of our churches now are focusing on raising up young people and helping them to hear the call—that gives me hope. We are becoming vital. I think that renewal will happen if we do the kinds of things you all are doing and talking about as New Adapters.

Mike: I was twenty-seven and Adam was twenty-five when we started out in ministry. Two young kids who were naïve. I remember my district superintendent telling me I was naïve, which was a good thing. I'm glad I was naïve. I thought, when you get there, when you finally get to pastor a church, just keep speaking the truth, keep speaking the truth.

Adam: I agree with Mike that if the movement remains resistant to change, there is a certain portion that will die off by slow decline. But I see all these new young ministries emerging, and I believe that God will use them to do something new. The Church of the Resurrection is not all that old. It started in 1990. It may be seen now as a venerable, established congregation, but in the big scheme of things it is relatively new. And in many respects, I hope there is always something "new" going on. We must remember that God does new things all around us, all the time. And I think God's going to continue doing that. Mike and I want to spend the last of our days not just collecting a pension check but also fanning the flames of that kind of revival in the Methodist movement.